Cambridge Elements ≡

Elements in Ethics
edited by
Ben Eggleston
University of Kansas
Dale E. Miller
Old Dominion University

T0286988

MOORE'S ETHICS

William H. Shaw
San José State University

CAMBRIDGE
UNIVERSITY PRESS

CAMBRIDGE
UNIVERSITY PRESS

University Printing House, Cambridge CB2 8BS, United Kingdom

One Liberty Plaza, 20th Floor, New York, NY 10006, USA

477 Williamstown Road, Port Melbourne, VIC 3207, Australia

314–321, 3rd Floor, Plot 3, Splendor Forum, Jasola District Centre,
New Delhi – 110025, India

79 Anson Road, #06–04/06, Singapore 079906

Cambridge University Press is part of the University of Cambridge.

It furthers the University's mission by disseminating knowledge in the pursuit of
education, learning, and research at the highest international levels of excellence.

www.cambridge.org
Information on this title: www.cambridge.org/9781108706544
DOI: 10.1017/9781108581295

© William H. Shaw 2020

First published 2020

A catalogue record for this publication is available from the British Library.

ISBN 978-1-108-70654-4 Paperback
ISSN 2516-4031 (online)
ISSN 2516-4023 (print)

Moore's Ethics

Elements in Ethics

DOI: 10.1017/9781108581295
First published online: August 2020

William H. Shaw
San José State University

Author for correspondence: William H. Shaw, bill.shaw@sjsu.edu

Abstract: This Element critically surveys the full range of G. E. Moore's ethical thought, including: (1) his rejection of naturalism in favor of the view that "good" designates a simple, indefinable property, which cannot be identified with or reduced to any other property; (2) his understanding of intrinsic value, his doctrine of organic wholes, his repudiation of hedonism, and his substantive account of the most important goods and evils; and (3) his critique of egoism and subjectivism and his elaboration of a nonhedonistic variant of utilitarianism that, among other things, creatively blends aspects of act- and rule-oriented versions of that theory.

Keywords: Moore, nonnaturalism, intrinsic value, organic wholes, utilitarianism

ISBNs: 9781108706544 (PB), 9781108581295 (OC)
ISSNs: 2516-4031 (online), 2516-4023 (print)

Contents

Introduction

G. E. Moore (1873–1958) was a central figure in early twentieth-century philosophy. Along with Russell and Wittgenstein, he pioneered analytic philosophy, and his argumentative technique, his intellectual example, and his characteristic philosophical concerns shaped the way several generations of philosophers approached their discipline. As a result, Moore's influence is difficult to exaggerate. Even if few contemporary philosophers self-consciously adhere to any distinctively Moorean tenets or methods, his legacy is deeply and permanently embedded in English-language philosophy. This is particularly true in ethics, where no philosopher had a greater impact in the first half of the twentieth century than did Moore (Darwall, 1989: 366; Baldwin, 1993: xxxvii; Horgan and Timmons, 2006: 1).

His *Principia Ethica* of 1903, arguably "the first work in analytical ethical philosophy" (Darwall, 2006: 18), restructured the field, and until the publication of John Rawls's *A Theory of Justice* in 1971, no single work in ethics was to have repercussions as profound. In *Principia* Moore undertook to formulate the basic questions of ethics with precision, to clarify the differences among them, and to define the fundamental concepts involved in, and specify the procedures appropriate to, answering them. He paid particular attention to the concept of goodness, famously rejecting any naturalistic account of it in favor of the view that it represents a simple, indefinable, and unanalyzable property. Largely because of *Principia*, for a half century metaethical disputes over the nature of moral judgment, the meaning of moral language, and the possibility, if any, of justifying ethical propositions dominated moral philosophy.

Moore's objectives in *Principia*, however, were not exclusively or primarily metaethical. There and in his *Ethics* of 1912, he also wanted to address two substantive questions: What kinds of things are good in themselves? and What kinds of actions ought we to perform? Accordingly, this survey of Moore's ethical thought examines not only his metaethical nonnaturalism (Section 1) but also his value theory, including his doctrine of organic wholes, his repudiation of hedonism, and his distinctive account of the most important goods and evils (Sections 2 and 3), and his thinking about right and wrong – in particular, his critique of egoism and subjectivism and his elaboration of a nonhedonistic variant of utilitarianism and the implications it has for individual conduct (Sections 4 and 5). Because in recent decades metaethics has ceased to rule moral philosophy, the relevance and importance of these often-neglected aspects of Moore's ethical thought have only increased. In particular, Moore's development of a normative theory that shares the consequentialism of classical utilitarianism while abandoning its value theory, that is sensitive to the limits of our knowledge, and that stresses the importance of adherence to rules while retaining an act-consequentialist criterion of right is more pertinent than ever.

1 The Meaning of "Good"

"It appears to me," Moore writes in the opening sentence of *Principia Ethica*, "that in Ethics, as in all other philosophical studies, the difficulties and disagreements of which its history are full, are mainly due to a very simple cause: namely, to the attempt to answer questions, without first discovering precisely *what* question it is you desire to answer" (33).[1] As a result, philosophers are "constantly endeavoring to prove that 'Yes' or 'No' will answer questions, to which *neither* answer is correct, owing to the fact that what they have before their minds is not one question, but several, to some of which the true answer is 'No,' to others 'Yes'" (33). In *Principia* Moore aspires to a higher standard of clarity and analytic rigor.

In particular, he wants to address two questions, both of which are central to moral philosophy but which, he believes, have been confused with one another or with other questions (33–4, 166). The first is, What ought to exist for its own sake – that is, what are the things that have intrinsic value or are good in themselves? Second is the question, What ought we to do – that is, what actions are we either permitted or required to perform? The first question is more basic, Moore believes, because we cannot know what good conduct is or what we ought to aim at without knowing what is good. "Nothing is more certain," he writes, "from an ethical point of view, than that some things are bad and others good; the object of Ethics is, indeed, in chief part, to give you general rules whereby you may avoid the one and secure the other" (94). Knowing what is good, however, and what is not requires understanding what is meant by "good." That is, what property or quality are we attributing to something when we say that it is good? True, we often successfully use a word or a concept, or correctly identify the things that possess a certain property, even if we cannot give a fully satisfactory definition or account of the concept or property in question. Moore acknowledges this, but he believes that if we don't know what "good" means, then "the rest of Ethics is as good as useless from the point of view of systematic knowledge." In particular, our "*most general* ethical judgments" are unlikely to be valid, and we won't understand what counts as evidence for any ethical judgment (57, 192–3).

---

[1] Parenthesized page numbers in the text are from *Principia Ethica* (Moore 1993b) unless preceded by an "E," in which case they refer to Moore's *Ethics* (Moore 2005a). Page references to other works by Moore are preceded by date and to the work of other authors by name and date.

Moore thinks, then, that "the most fundamental question in all Ethics" is "how 'good' is to be defined" (57, 192). In asking what is meant by "good," however, Moore is not concerned with its proper usage as determined by custom (58). Nor is he calling for a dictionary definition or an account of the different ways the word "good" can be used, and indeed he acknowledges that it can have different meanings (E 82; 1962: 89–90). He is interested in the concept of goodness or the object, idea, or property that the adjective "good" stands for when used in ethical contexts – for example, when someone says that friendship is good or that pain is bad or asks whether pleasure is good in itself or has intrinsic value. What, then, is goodness? What does it mean for something to be good?

Moore's answer is famous: "Good" is indefinable. "If I am asked 'What is good?' my answer is that good is good, and that is the end of the matter. Or if asked 'How is good to be defined?' my answer is that it cannot be defined, and that is all I have to say about it" (58). This response may seem disappointing, but Moore thought it had an important implication. If "good" cannot be defined – if it is an unanalyzable concept – then meaning alone cannot settle the truth or falsity of propositions about what is good or bad. Any such propositions are therefore synthetic, not analytic; that is, they are substantive assertions and never simply definitional or conceptual truths. This is important because, Moore thinks, philosophers frequently base their claims about what is good or bad on implicit or explicit appeals to definition. They confuse the question "What things are good in themselves?" with the question "What is meant by 'good'?" (89–90, 109–10). But if good is indefinable, he writes, then nobody can foist on us propositions about what is good "on the pretence that this is 'the very meaning of the word'" (58–9). We approach questions of what is good or bad with a more open mind, Moore believes, if we realize that this is not something that can be settled by definition.

Moore draws a parallel with "yellow." Like it, "good" is a simple notion – too simple to be defined or analyzed. This does not imply that we don't know what yellowness or goodness is or that we cannot recognize that something is "yellow" or "good." To the contrary, we know perfectly well that the bananas in front of us are yellow or that kindness is good. But what we cannot do is define those terms or analyze or break them down into component parts. On Moore's view, "definitions which describe the real nature of the object or notion denoted by a word . . . are only possible when the object or notion is something complex" (59). Like "yellow," however, "good" does not refer to an object composed of parts that we can substitute in our minds when thinking of it. "The most important sense of 'definition,'" Moore writes, "is that in which a definition states what are the parts which invariably compose a certain whole; and in this sense 'good' has no definition because it is simple and has no parts" (61). Many other objects of thought are equally incapable of definition for the same reason. They "are the ultimate terms by reference to which whatever *is* capable of definition must be defined" (61). Although "good" is indefinable, nevertheless "we are all aware of a certain simple quality," and it is this, and nothing else, that "we mainly mean by the term 'good'" (90).

1.1 The Naturalistic Fallacy

Goodness is a property of certain natural objects or states of affairs, but it is not itself a natural property. It is not part of the natural world. It is not a constituent part of any physical object or any real state of affairs; that is to say, any physical object or state of affairs can be fully and completely described without mentioning its goodness or badness. When this point is understood, it seems less odd for Moore to contend, as he does, that the adjective "good" belongs to that "class of objects or properties of objects, which certainly do not exist in time, are not therefore parts of Nature, and which, in fact, do not *exist* at all" (161; cf. 93, 176). Various good things do exist, of course. However, only these things – the things that are good – and not goodness itself can exist in time, that is, have duration and begin or cease to exist. Only they can be objects of perception. In contending that the property designated by "good" does not exist in a material sense, Moore is not maintaining that it is imaginary. Goodness is like the number two. "Two and two *are* four. But that does not mean that either two or four exists" (162). There can be two real things – two hats, two cars, or two shoes – but "twoness" itself is not an object that exists.

Thus, when Moore denies "that 'good' *must* denote some *real* property of things," he is not denying that it designates something (191). His point, rather, is that what it denotes is not a natural or empirical aspect of a thing. When we see that something is good, its goodness is "not a property which we can take up in our hands, or separate from it even by the most delicate scientific instruments" (175). As a nonnatural property, goodness lies beyond the province of psychology or the natural sciences; in ascribing goodness to an object, we do not describe the object at all (92; 1952: 591). It follows from the intrinsic nature of an object, but it is not one of its intrinsic properties; it does not make the object what it is (1993a: 296). Nor does "good" designate some supersensible property or refer to some metaphysical reality. "Any truth which asserts 'This is good in itself' is quite unique in kind ... it cannot be reduced to any assertion about reality, and therefore must remain unaffected by any conclusions we reach about the nature of [physical or metaphysical] reality" (165; cf. 174).

Although "good" denotes a nonnatural property, and thus ethics is not a purely empirical enterprise, as was said above the things that are good do exist in the natural world. The adjective *good* must not be confused with the things to which the adjective applies, and those things are real existing objects or states of affairs. To say, for example, that "friendship is good" is not to define "good" as "friendship," but to attribute a property, namely, goodness, to something that does or can exist, namely, friendship. Although we cannot define "good," it does not follow from this "that *the* good, that which is good, is thus indefinable" (60). We can define the good by enumeration or extension, that is, by listing or describing those things that are good.

To attempt to define "good" and thus fail to recognize that it denotes a unique, indefinable, and unanalyzable quality, which is not equivalent to any other property, is to commit what Moore famously called the "naturalistic fallacy." This fallacy "consists in identifying the simple notion which we mean by 'good' with some other notion" (109) – in particular, in contending "that good *means* nothing but some simple or complex notion, that can be defined in terms of natural qualities" (125). In trying to define what cannot be defined, the fallacy rests on a failure "to perceive that the notion of intrinsic value is simple and unique" (222; cf. 111). It is because goodness is frequently but erroneously identified with some natural or empirically determinable object or property like pleasure or that which is approved or desired that Moore calls the fallacy in question the naturalistic fallacy. But metaphysical theories of ethics commit the same fallacy when they identify good with some supersensible property or reality (91, 164–5). Goodness is distinct from any other property, whether empirical or metaphysical – that, Moore later stressed in an unpublished manuscript, was the point he was trying to drive home in *Principia* (13, 15).

There are, Moore contends, only two alternatives to the proposition that "good" denotes something simple and indefinable: Either it stands for "a complex, a given whole, about the correct analysis of which there may be disagreement; or else it means nothing at all, and there is no such subject as Ethics" (66). Let us begin with the second possibility. The passage in question is difficult to interpret, but what Moore seems to have in mind is not that "good" would be literally meaningless, but rather that if goodness were identical with some simple, natural property like pleasure, then "good" would lack any distinct or independent meaning. But "good" does have, he thinks, just such a meaning; it refers to a unique property or characteristic of things. If we ask whether something is good, we are not asking, for example, whether it is pleasant, and certainly if we ask whether pleasure is good, we are not wondering whether pleasure is pleasant. To the contrary, "good" has a distinct meaning for people even if they do not recognize the respect in which it is distinct: "Whenever [one] thinks of 'intrinsic value,' or 'intrinsic worth,' or says that a thing 'ought to exist,' he has before his mind the unique object – the unique property of things – which I mean by 'good.' Everybody is constantly aware of this notion, although he may never become aware at all that it is different from other notions of which he is also aware" (68). Even if "good" can be used in different ways in different contexts ("she has a good credit score" or "chocolate sorbet tastes good"), it still has this core ethical meaning (1952: 554).

1.2 The Open-Question Argument

Turning to the other alternative – that "good" designates some complex property – Moore defends his contrary view that it is simple, indefinable, and unanalyzable by advancing what has come to be called the "open-question argument." The argument is short and straightforward: "Whatever definition [of good] be offered, it may be always asked, with significance, of the complex so defined, whether it is itself good" (67). Although Moore is attacking definitions that identify good with some complex property, his argument applies equally well to definitions that equate it with some simple property. To understand the argument, suppose someone defines "good" as – to pick some possible examples – (1) pleasure, (2) that which promotes the survival of the species, (3) what God wants for us, or (4) what one would desire upon informed reflection. It is still perfectly coherent, Moore is arguing, for one to say, "I know that this is pleasurable (or what God wants for us or what an informed person would desire upon reflection), but is it good?" The very fact that a person can intelligibly ask whether a certain pleasure is good or whether what promotes the survival of the species is good – the very fact that these are open or meaningful questions – shows that we have a different notion in mind when we ask of something whether it is good than we do when we ask whether it is pleasurable or promotes the survival of the species or is what an informed person would desire.

By contrast, suppose someone said, "I know that Charles is a widower, but was he ever married?" That is not an open question. To the contrary, it shows only that the speaker has not grasped the meaning of the word "widower." Of course, not every definition is as trivial as this. For example, many philosophers have held that "knowledge" means "justified true belief," so that one knows X if and only if one believes X, X is indeed true, and one is justified in believing X. Although few epistemologists today accept this definition without qualification, assume, for the sake of discussion, that it is basically correct. If we have never thought about the meaning of "knowledge" before, this definition will come as new information to us and so it might seem to us an open question whether it is correct. But the more we think about it, the more convinced we may become that "justified true belief" encapsulates what we mean by "knowledge." If so, asking whether knowledge is justified true belief ceases to be an open question. When it comes to "good," however, the situation is different. When we reflect on any proposed definition of it, we will see, as we mull it over, that it fails to capture what we mean when we call something "good."

If we acknowledge that goodness is indefinable and, in particular, that it is distinct from any natural or metaphysical property, then, Moore believes, we will avoid the tangles that most ethical theories find themselves in. We will be less likely to err in our search for those things that are good because we will understand that this is not something that can be settled by definition. Moreover, if we try to rest our ethical principles on a definition of good, we cannot logically defend them. All we can do is arbitrarily assert (or deny) that "good" really means such-and-such. What is worse, we shall "be inclined either to misunderstand our opponent's arguments or to cut them short with the reply, 'This is not an open question: the very meaning of the word decides it; no one can think otherwise except through confusion'" (72).

Does the open-question objection, then, convincingly refute naturalism? A long-standing criticism of Moore's argument is that even if it squelches this or that proposed naturalistic definition of good (as, say, pleasure, or what we would desire if fully informed), we cannot generalize from this and jump to the conclusion that any definition that someone might come up with will succumb to it. But Moore can be seen, not as trying to establish this conclusion by induction, but rather as laying down a challenge: Try to find a definition of good that gets around the open-question objection; you won't succeed. As we examine various proposals, he thinks, we will come to realize that "good" escapes definition or analysis. Of course, it is possible that we might be surprised, as we were in the case of "knowledge," by some new definition that we had never thought of before and that captures exactly what we have in mind when we call something good. But this seems unlikely. The concept of goodness has evaluative force; to describe a thing or state of affairs as good is to commend it, to attribute value to it, to say of it that it is better for it to exist than not to exist. And if something like this is correct, then no descriptive definition can fully capture the meaning of good.

Most philosophers today agree with Moore that "good" is not synonymous with or conceptually equivalent to any nonmoral concept. Still, it might possibly be the case that the property of goodness is, in fact, identical to some natural property X even if "good" does not mean "X." If so, then some kind of nondefinitional or nonanalytic naturalism would be true. Some contemporary philosophers defend this position, which seems safe from the open-question argument, by drawing analogies with scientific knowledge. Consider salt, for example. Salt, we now know, is NaCl, but this was a discovery about salt. It was not a definitional truth, which we learned by reflecting on our concepts, because "salt" and "NaCl" have different meanings. Likewise, these contemporary naturalists urge, goodness is (or might be) identical to or reducible to some natural property or properties even if this is not an analytic or conceptual truth.

The tenability of this proposal and, more specifically, the analogy with science are matters of debate. For one thing, our prescientific concept of salt left open for empirical investigation the true nature of the substance that has the properties we associate with salt. But it is doubtful that our concept of goodness is similarly incomplete, waiting to be filled out by further research. Moore himself did not explicitly consider nonanalytic naturalism, but its contemporary critics reject it on broadly Moorean grounds, arguing that no account of goodness or any other ethical property that reduces it to or identifies it with some natural property, whether by definition or otherwise, can capture its normative (or commendatory or action-guiding) force. Even if everything that is X is good, and the only things that are good are X, still the property of being good would seem to be distinct from the property of being X. In other words, even if it were true that X and only X makes things good, their coextensiveness would not entail that X-ness and goodness are the very same thing (Parfit, 2011–7, III: 71–2, 75–83).

Moore believed that most earlier writers in ethics were guilty of the naturalistic fallacy – of identifying goodness with some natural or metaphysical property – and he devotes nearly three chapters of *Principia* to showing how thinkers as diverse as Aristotle, Spinoza, Leibniz, Kant, Bentham, Mill, Green, and Spencer rested their ethical theories on some implicit or explicit claim about what good means. Henry Sidgwick, the great utilitarian thinker and one of Moore's teachers, is the only philosopher acknowledged by Moore to have understood that good is unanalyzable. But although the writers Moore criticizes do link the good to different natural or supersensible properties, it is far from clear – perhaps even to these writers themselves – whether they are doing so on the basis of a definition of "good." As Moore himself stresses, one does not commit the naturalistic fallacy merely by identifying the kinds of thing that are good or claiming that X is the only good. However, a substantive assertion about what is good requires some sort of support or argument to back it up, and Moore thought, correctly or incorrectly, that these writers were not offering arguments but passing off their views about the good as definitional truths.

Whatever the merits of Moore's critique of these philosophers, *Principia Ethica* profoundly influenced the course of metaethics in the twentieth century. Before too long it was recognized as a classic, and many philosophers found Moore's bracing critique of naturalism fully convincing. However, his doctrine that ethical knowledge involves the apprehension of a sui generis, nonnatural property (namely, goodness) never found as much favor. Many philosophers were uncomfortable with the idea that we are able, somehow, to intuit, recognize, or apprehend certain nonnatural ethical properties or to grasp in a nonempirical way the truth of propositions referring to those properties. This can be seen as an epistemological worry. They were also puzzled about the ontological status of nonnatural properties and how, exactly, they are related to the natural (or descriptive or nonmoral) properties on which they supervene. Moore thought that if two things have the same empirical properties, then they will be good or bad to the same degree. Their goodness can differ only if their empirical or descriptive properties differ. But how, then, do those natural properties give rise to nonnatural properties? This can be seen as a metaphysical worry.

Worries like these may have reflected inaccurate understandings of Moore, who did not believe that ethical knowledge was the product of a distinct kind of cognition (36) and avoided attributing some special reality to nonnatural properties (162–3). Nevertheless, they led some philosophers, not to try to breathe life into naturalism, but rather to adopt *noncognitivism*, generally understood as the position that distinctively ethical discourse is not cognitive at all – that is, that ethical statements are neither true nor false. Rather than being propositions with truth value (for example, the proposition that X has the property of goodness), ethical statements are an expression of attitude or emotion or some kind of prescription or endorsement. To say "X is good" is not to say something that is either true or false but, rather, to recommend, endorse, prescribe, or express some other positive attitude toward X. Noncognitivists accept Moore's open-question argument, but reject his cognitivism, his belief that there are true ethical propositions and that we can know some of them.

Noncognitivism dominated Anglo-American philosophy in the middle of the twentieth century and still has influential and philosophically sophisticated advocates. But these days many philosophers reject it, largely because moral discourse and the structure of moral language seem to presuppose that ethical statements (e.g., "torture is wrong") make claims about the way things are, claims that can be true or false and are not just prescriptions ("don't torture") or expressions of attitude ("I'm against torture").[2] Some of these philosophers favor some kind of nonanalytic naturalism and seek to show that moral properties and moral facts, even if not definitionally or conceptually equivalent to

---

[2] To be sure, noncognitivists try to explain why we are justified in acting as if moral judgments had truth value even though, on their view, they don't. So-called moral error theorists (Mackie 1977) take a different tack. They grant that moral judgments have truth value, but contend that all such judgments are false.

natural properties and facts, are nevertheless identical to them. Other contemporary cognitivists are, like Moore, nonnaturalists. They believe that we have moral knowledge but that moral properties and facts cannot be reduced to, or identified with, natural or nonethical properties or facts. Thus, metaethics since *Principia* can be seen as an increasingly intricate and sophisticated three-way debate among proponents of naturalism, of nonnaturalism, and of noncognitivism – a debate set off by Moore's open-question argument.

2 Intrinsic Goodness

Throughout his writings, Moore emphasizes that judgments about goodness divide into two types: judgments about whether something is good in itself and judgments about whether it is good as a means – that is, as a cause or necessary condition of something else that is good in itself. "The nature of these two species of universal ethical judgments is extremely different," he states in *Principia*, "and a great part of the difficulties, which are met with in ordinary ethical speculation, are due to the failure to distinguish them clearly" (73; cf. 75). In particular, we need to avoid the error of supposing that something that is a means to good and, indeed, which may even seem necessary here and now for the existence of anything good, is therefore good in itself (236). Appreciating the difference between these two types of judgments, Moore contends, is absolutely crucial if one is to analyze and answer correctly potentially ambiguous questions like "What should we aim at?" or "Is it right to act this way?" To answer such questions, "we must know *both* what degree of intrinsic value different things have, *and* how these different things may be obtained" (77).

Judgments about goodness as a means are essentially causal and predictive. They assert that some action, thing, or state of affairs will have certain effects. However, because circumstances vary, it is virtually impossible that a given thing or action will always produce the same result. Indeed, "a thing which has good effects under some circumstances may have bad effects under others" (78–9). The most we can hope to know is that a certain result "generally follows" this kind of thing (74). And even this generalization will hold only if circumstances are generally the same, and although this may be so for a particular age or at a certain stage of society, what is generally true at one period may be generally false at another. Moreover, to judge that something is generally a means to good we need to know not only that it usually does some good but also that the balance of good will generally be greater than if one had done something else instead (74).

By contrast, judgments that certain kinds of things or states of affairs are good in themselves – that they are intrinsically valuable – are not causal or empirical judgments. Nor does their truth vary with the circumstances.[3] Indeed, they are logically independent of any truths about the way the world is (1903b: 116). Furthermore, if these judgments are true, then they are universally true (215). This entails that if one instance of a thing has intrinsic value, then necessarily all other instances of it do, too. This is because, as Moore sees it, intrinsic value depends only on the intrinsic nature of the thing that possesses it, and the intrinsic nature of a thing does not change with the situation or circumstances (1993a: 286; 1952: 603). Its external relations, that is, the relations it has to other things – for example, that somebody desires it – do not change its basic nature. The value that a thing has in itself hangs only on the nature of the thing itself.

2.1 Organic Wholes

Complicating the analysis of intrinsic value is what Moore, appropriating some neo-Hegelian terminology for his own purposes, calls the principle of "organic wholes" (or, alternatively, "organic unities" or "organic relations"). The principle may be explained as follows. A thing (which will itself be intrinsically good, intrinsically bad, or indifferent) can occur as part of a whole, which includes other things that are good, bad, or indifferent. This whole, in turn, will have an intrinsic value that is positive, negative, or neutral. Now it might seem obvious that the value of this whole must equal the value of its parts. Moore, however, denies this, upholding instead the apparent "paradox" that "the value of such a whole bears no regular proportion to the sum of the values of its parts" (79). This, then, is the principle of organic wholes.

The principle plays an important role in Moore's account of the things that are intrinsically good and bad, and both *Principia* and *Ethics* affirm it. He sees it as one of the least appreciated but most significant principles of ethics because, if we neglect it, we are bound to go astray when we compare the relative values of different things. Although Moore affirms the "principle ... that the intrinsic value of a whole is neither identical with nor proportional to the sum of the values of its parts," he is more accurately understood as denying that there must be, or that there generally is, such an identity or proportion, rather than as asserting that such an identity or proportion could never obtain (233). Accordingly, not all wholes are organic wholes – organic wholes being defined as those wholes the intrinsic value of which is not equal to the sum of the values of their parts. This point makes less pressing the objection that Moore never tells us how to individuate wholes or what makes something a whole in the first place (as opposed, say, to a mere collection or grouping of things). We can still identify some things as organic wholes (because their value does not equal

---

[3] For an argument to the contrary and Moore's response to it, see 1952: 618–20.

the sum of the values of their parts) even if it is left vague how to distinguish among different possible wholes or how to delineate wholes from nonwholes.

The principle of organic wholes has a variety of implications for Moore. It implies, in particular, (a) that the value of a whole composed of two good things may be immensely greater than the sum of their two values, (b) that a whole composed of a good thing and an indifferent thing may have a value far greater than the good thing possesses by itself, (c) that two bad things or a bad thing and an indifferent thing can form a whole much worse than the sum of its parts, and (d) that indifferent things can form a whole that has great value, either positive or negative (79). Consciousness of a beautiful object illustrates the last point. It seems intrinsically valuable, yet it is a whole comprising two things – an object and consciousness of something – neither of which has much, if any, value by itself. On the one hand, beautiful objects of which no one is conscious have little or no value; on the other, consciousness occurs as part of a whole whenever we are aware of anything, yet many of these wholes are indifferent or even positively bad (79–80). It will always be problematic, then, to ask which parts or constituents of a whole are the source of its value (or disvalue). The answer may well be none of them.

The parts that make up an organic whole are necessary conditions of its existence; without them, it would not be what it is. But a part is not to be confused with something that is a means to bringing about that whole. The necessity of a part to its whole is independent of the laws of nature, whereas the necessity involved when X is said to be a necessary means to Y is natural or causal necessity (80–1). If the laws of nature were different, then Y might have existed without X's having occurred. Furthermore, a means does not itself affect the intrinsic value of the object it brings about. By contrast, the existence of the whole includes, as a matter of conceptual necessity, the existence of the part; remove the part and you no longer have the whole. This fact does not, however, entail that a part must have more intrinsic value than does a means or even that it must have any intrinsic value at all. Indeed,

> the part of a valuable whole retains exactly the same value when it is, as when it is not, a part of that whole. . . . Its value is not any greater, when it is part of a far more valuable whole; and if it had no value by itself, it has none still. . . . We are not then justified in asserting that one and the same thing is under some circumstances intrinsically good, and under others not so. . . . And yet we are justified in asserting that it is far more desirable that a certain thing should exist under some circumstances than under others; namely when other things will exist in such relations to it as to form a more valuable whole. (81)

A thing's intrinsic value always remains the same, whether it is a means to, or even part of, a whole that is more or less valuable than it is.

How does one determine the intrinsic value of something, whether a whole or a part? How are we to decide whether there really are wholes the value of which is not proportional to the value of their parts? The only way, Moore thinks, is the method of isolation. Moore implicitly relied on this method in assessing the relative value of the contemplation of beauty and the parts that constitute it, and he appeals to it throughout *Principia* and *Ethics*. When employing the method, one is engaging in a thought experiment. This consists in "considering what value we should attach to [the thing], if it existed in absolute isolation, stripped of all its usual accompaniments" (142; cf. E 34, 1962: 93). Something is intrinsically good if and only if its existence by itself would be good, so to determine its intrinsic value, we have to imagine it existing by itself without the circumstances that usually accompany it or the consequences that usually flow from it, and then judge whether its bare existence would be good, bad, or indifferent. Similarly, one determines the relative degree of value of different things by comparing the value that attaches to the isolated existence of each.

Is the method sound? Both imagining and assessing a thing apart from its usual context and consequences may be harder to do than it seems, and various extraneous factors could well affect one's judgments of intrinsic value. On the other hand, if goodness is an objective feature of certain things or states of affairs but is not something that can be measured or tested empirically, it is difficult to see any alternative to the method of isolation. By definition, intrinsic value is the value that a thing possesses in itself. To judge this, all we can do, it seems, is to think about the thing by itself, apart from its usual causes, context, and consequences, and to try to appraise, as carefully and impartially as we can, what value it would then have.

2.2 Refinements and Elaborations

In addition to identifying the value of an organic whole, Moore says, we may also need to consider its value "on the whole." This is "the sum of the value which it possesses *as a whole, together with* the intrinsic values which may belong to any of its parts" (263). Suppose, then, that entity A with intrinsic value a and entity B with intrinsic value b form an organic whole C and that this whole has intrinsic value c. This is C's value "as a whole," which is not necessarily, the principle of organic wholes instructs us, simply the sum of a and b. Moore is now drawing a distinction between this and C's value "on the whole." Its value on the whole is c (its value as a whole) plus a and b (the value that A and B have independently of C).

This seems like double counting. If A and B form an organic whole, what rationale can there be for adding A's and B's independent values to the value of that whole – that is, the values they have apart from the whole? The answer is that doing so allows Moore to deal with a problem posed by retributive (or what he calls "vindictive") punishment as well as by certain "mixed" virtues like compassion (262–3, 265). Like some other philosophers, Moore believes that the just punishment of evil conduct is good in itself and not merely valuable as a means to other goods, such as deterrence or rehabilitation. Even though wickedness (the evil action) and pain (the punishment) are both bad things, that evil be punished is desirable for its own sake and certainly far better than evil going unrequited. Similarly, compassion is an intrinsically good thing, but there can be no compassion without the suffering to which it responds. If suffering exists, then it is good that it be compassioned, and if there is wickedness, then it is good that it be punished. However, although compassion and just punishment are good in themselves, in neither case do we want to say that it is good that suffering exists in order that there be compassion or good that there are wicked deeds so that they can be justly punished. These states of affairs – wickedness plus its condign punishment; suffering plus compassionate responses to it – are not good overall or on the whole; that is, the world would have been better without them even though compassion and just punishment are good in themselves.

Thus, the distinction between something's value "as a whole" and its value "on the whole" solves a difficulty for Moore. But the distinction might strike one as artificial and ad hoc because its only purpose seems to be to preserve the assumption that punishment is intrinsically, and not just instrumentally, good and that compassion and certain other virtues are inherently good, not just good because of their results. Those assumptions rest on intuitions that might be challenged.

In *Ethics* Moore suggests a further distinction between "intrinsically good," on the one hand, and "ultimately good" or "good for its own sake," on the other. Both the former and latter labels appropriately "apply to things whose existence *would* be good, even if they existed quite alone," but there is a difference between them (E 36). A whole that is intrinsically good may, as we have seen, have parts that are not intrinsically good – that is, that would not be good if they existed by themselves. But something that is ultimately good or good for its own sake contains no such parts.[4] "We may, in short," Moore writes,

> divide intrinsically good things into two classes: namely (1) those which, while as wholes they are intrinsically good, nevertheless contain some parts which are not intrinsically good; and (2) those, which either have no parts at

---

[4] Ross (1930: 69) suggests that "good throughout" would express Moore's meaning better than "ultimately good" or "good for its own sake."

all, or, if they have any, have none but what are themselves intrinsically good.
(E 37)

This distinction illuminates a point about hedonistic utilitarianism. That theory
holds that pleasure is the only ultimate good but not that pleasure is the only
thing intrinsically good (E 36–7). Rather, utilitarianism asserts that wholes that
contain an excess of pleasure over pain are intrinsically good and that one whole
is intrinsically better than another whenever it contains a greater balance of
pleasure over pain.

Even more usefully, Moore differentiates between (1) whether, and in what
degree, a thing is intrinsically good or bad, as revealed by the method of
isolation, and (2) whether, and in what degree, it is capable of adding to or
subtracting from the intrinsic value of a whole of which it is part. Something that
is not intrinsically good might be good in this second sense if it adds to the value
of many intrinsically good wholes. A further question is (3) whether, and in
what degree, something is useful and has good effects (or is harmful and has bad
effects) (E 130). These are three discrete issues. Distinguishing among them is
important because the degree of something's goodness or badness in any one of
these three senses bears no fixed relation to its degree of goodness or badness in
the others.

3 The Things That Are Good

Before turning to Moore's account of the most important intrinsic goods, we
need to examine his critique of hedonism. Hedonism is the theory of good
associated with classical utilitarianism – that is, with the utilitarianism of
Bentham, Mill,[5] Sidgwick, and the utilitarians of Moore's day – and it is
Moore's utter and unequivocal repudiation of hedonism while nevertheless
adhering to the consequentialist normative structure of utilitarianism that is
distinctive of his theory of right and wrong.

3.1 Against Hedonism

Hedonism maintains that "pleasure *alone* is good as an end or in itself" (114)
or, in the terminology of *Ethics*, that all pleasure and nothing but pleasure is
"ultimately good" or "good for its own sake" (E 37).[6] Likewise, nothing is
ultimately bad or bad for its own sake except pain. The hedonist does not deny

---

[5] Because Mill distinguished among pleasures in terms of quality, many commentators maintain
that he in effect abandoned hedonism. But this was not Mill's own view of what he was doing.

[6] Moore takes pleasure to be a special sort of sensation (64). In *Principia* Moore argues that what
hedonists should value is not pleasure but, rather, consciousness of pleasure (139–42). But he
frequently ignores this somewhat problematic distinction, and *Ethics* pays no attention to it.

that things other than pleasure, such as beauty, knowledge, or friendship may be good, but they are good only as means to pleasure or for the sake of pleasure (115). Nonhedonists might concede that pleasure is intrinsically valuable or, at least, that some pleasures are intrinsically valuable, but they reject the idea that it is the only thing that is or can be good in itself. Moore frequently refers to hedonism as an "ethical" principle, but hedonism is compatible with different principles about how one ought to act. It is a doctrine about value rather than conduct, about what is worthwhile rather than about what it is right for us to do.

Bentham, Mill, and Sidgwick were hedonists. They equated pleasure with happiness and pain with unhappiness, and they were concerned with happiness because they implicitly identified it with well-being, that is, with what is good for people or makes their lives go well for them. The welfare or well-being of sentient creatures is what they were seeking to maximize. In principle, hedonism as a theory of what is good differs from hedonism as an account of well-being, but if (as utilitarians think) well-being is all that matters, then this difference more or less evaporates.

Although utilitarians today also seek to maximize well-being, they often take a broader view of happiness, distinguishing it from pleasure, or believe that there is more to well-being than happiness, or both. One influential account of what is good for people holds that happiness or well-being consists, not in pleasure, but in the satisfaction of one's desires, that is, in one's getting what one wants (or, alternatively, what one would want under certain conditions). Such a position had yet to be clearly articulated in Moore's time, but *Principia Ethica* touches on a closely related idea when it quotes T. H. Green as stating that "*the* common characteristic of the good is that it satisfies some desire." This seems to imply that "being good is *identical* with satisfying desire" or that "'good' is merely another name for 'desire-satisfying'" (189). If so, then Green manifestly commits the naturalistic fallacy.

Defining "good" as "desire-satisfying" obviously differs from defining it as pleasure. Nevertheless, there is a connection, Moore believes, between this definition and hedonistic utilitarianism because some utilitarians take that definition for granted and then go on to argue that because people desire only pleasure, then pleasure alone is good. Moore points to John Stuart Mill as an example. In Chapter IV of *Utilitarianism*, Mill famously held that pleasure can be shown to be desirable because and only because people do in fact desire it. By calling something desirable, Mill clearly means that it *ought* to be desired – that is, that it is good and not just something that is thought to be good or happens to be desired. As a result, Moore contends, Mill commits the naturalistic fallacy:

"he takes 'the desirable,' which he uses as a synonym for 'the good,' to *mean* what *can* be desired" (124).[7]

Moore thinks that most hedonists commit the naturalistic fallacy. Sidgwick is an exception. Moore praises him for being the only ethical writer to recognize and clearly state that "good" is indefinable. Sidgwick holds that the doctrine of hedonism cannot be proved true but rather must rest on an appeal to intuition – that is, "to the sober judgment of reflective persons" (Sidgwick, 1966: 400). Moore agrees that on this issue no strict proof is possible, but he thinks that, in Mill's phrase, "considerations may be presented capable of determining the intellect either to give or withhold its assent to the doctrine" (126; Mill, 1969: 208). Contrary to Sidgwick, though, Moore believes that these considerations lead one to reject hedonism.

Moore begins by challenging Sidgwick's contention that nothing can be good except in relation to human existence or at least to some consciousness or feeling. Sidgwick denies, for instance, the rationality of producing something beautiful if no human being could possibly contemplate it. Moore replies that he, for one, considers it perfectly rational to hold that a world of beautiful mountains, rivers, sunsets, and stars is better than a world that is "simply one heap of filth," even if no human being could ever see either world. Indeed, he asks, "would it not be well ... to do what we could to produce [the one world] rather than the other?" (135). Contrary to this, however, one might well doubt the reasonableness of sacrificing anything of significance in order to bring about the more beautiful world when neither will ever be seen, and as touched on earlier, elsewhere in *Principia* Moore himself concedes that the mere existence of beauty has value "so small as to be negligible, in comparison with that which attaches to the *consciousness* of beauty" (237–8; cf. 79).

Sidgwick affirms not only that nothing can be good except in relation to consciousness but furthermore that only pleasure is good for its own sake. In his view, for instance, knowing the truth or contemplating beauty is valuable only insofar as it directly or indirectly increases pleasure or diminishes pain. The contention that only pleasurable consciousness is ultimately valuable can, Sidgwick thinks, be reasonably well reconciled with our commonsense judgments. Moore thinks not. He recognizes, though, that the important issue is not the extent to which hedonism fits or fails to fit with common sense but, rather, whether (as mentioned above) it can be defended by an appeal to what Sidgwick calls our "intuitive judgment after due consideration of the question when fairly placed before it" (Sidgwick, 1966: 400). Sidgwick claims, and Moore denies,

---

[7] In fact, Mill writes that what people desire is "evidence" of what is desirable, which suggests, contrary to Moore, that he saw "desired" and "desirable" (or "good") as distinct concepts (Mill, 1969: 234).

that our intuitive judgment supports the claim that knowing the truth or contemplating beauty is valuable only insofar as it is accompanied by or results in pleasure.

As Moore sees it, Sidgwick errs in arguing from the premises (1) that pleasure seems to be a necessary constituent of all valuable wholes and (2) that the other constituents of these wholes do not seem to have value to the conclusion (3) that pleasure alone has value. This reasoning, Moore asserts, neglects the principle of organic wholes (144). Contrary to what he takes Sidgwick to be saying, Moore argues that even if we grant that contemplating beauty is valuable only when pleasurable, it does not follow that pleasure alone is what makes it valuable.

Sidgwick uses something like the method of isolation when he asks whether we would continue to value beauty, knowledge, freedom, and virtue if they involved no pleasure. Strip away the pleasurable consciousness that accompanies or follows from these things, Sidgwick is in effect saying, and you strip away their value. Moore rejoins, however, that Sidgwick applies the method of isolation to only one element of the whole he is considering. He has not isolated the important issue because he fails to address the following questions: "If consciousness of pleasure existed absolutely by itself, would a sober judgment be able to attribute much value to it? ... Could we accept, as a very good thing, that mere consciousness of pleasure, and absolutely nothing else, should exist, even in the greatest quantities?" (145). Moore is confident that the answer to these questions is no. "It seems quite plain," he writes,

> that we do regard as very desirable, many complicated states of mind in which the consciousness of pleasure is combined with consciousness of other things. ... If this is correct, then it follows that consciousness of pleasure is not the sole good, and that many other states, in which it is included as a part, are much better than it. (147)

Not only are some "enjoyments" more valuable than the pleasure they contain, even though without that pleasure they would have had no value, but also pleasure makes certain states of affairs positively bad (236–7, 262).

Many people, Moore believes, erroneously move from the plausible thought that no whole has intrinsic value unless it contains some pleasure to the conclusion that intrinsic value is always in proportion to the quantity of pleasure (E 124–5). Yet, Moore's case against hedonism mainly rests, not on this point or on the principle of organic unities, but rather on an appeal to several related, antihedonistic intuitions. Had Moore been a little clearer about this fact, he might perhaps have spent more time elaborating and defending these beliefs. They include the following: (1) that certain things are valuable in the absence of pleasure, (2) that a world of pleasure alone would have less value than some worlds with less pleasure, and (3) that certain complex mental states are much more valuable than the pleasure they contain. The truth of any of these would refute hedonism.

Moore's earlier example of two worlds, one beautiful, the other ugly, but both beyond human ken supports intuition 1. So does the putative intrinsic goodness of purely retributive punishment. But both these judgments are controversial, and Moore offers no other examples that support this intuition. Moore endorses intuition 2 more clearly and firmly, claiming in *Principia Ethica* that as a hedonist, Sidgwick would have to endorse "a heaven, in which there would be no more refined pleasures—no contemplation of beauty, no personal affections—but in which the greatest possible pleasure would be obtained by a perpetual indulgence in bestiality" (146–7). In a related vein, *Ethics* denies

> that a world in which absolutely nothing except pleasure existed—no knowledge, no love, no enjoyment of beauty, no moral qualities—must yet be intrinsically better—better worth creating—provided only that the total quantity of pleasure in it were the least bit greater than one in which all these things existed *as well as* pleasure. (E 123)

In support of intuition 3 – that certain complex mental states are more valuable than the pleasure they contain – Moore argues that to deny this

> involves our saying that, for instance, the state of mind of a drunkard, when he is intensely pleased with breaking crockery, is just as valuable, in itself—just as well worth having, as that of a man who is fully realizing all that is exquisite in the tragedy of *King Lear*, provided only the mere quantity of pleasure in both cases is the same. Such instances might be multiplied indefinitely, and it seems to me that they constitute a *reductio ad absurdum* of the view that intrinsic value is always in proportion to quantity of pleasure. (E 123–4; cf. 1903a: 359)

And elsewhere Moore goes so far as to doubt that an action producing "the greatest quantity of pleasure [but] wholly unaccompanied by any other result whatever" would be worth performing (1907–8: 450).

In response, hedonists like Sidgwick are likely to query how people could possibly be as happy or find as much pleasure in living lives devoid of knowledge, love, or aesthetic enjoyment as they would in living lives with those things. Likewise, to suppose a world where bestiality brings humanity greater satisfaction than does human love and affection is to imagine a world in which our nature is so altered that it is not clear what import our intuitions about such a world would have. Finally, hedonists will maintain that even if the mental state of the drunkard and that of the playgoer are equally valuable because equally pleasurable, there are many reasons for believing that the former's life will be less pleasant overall. These points may not fully blunt Moore's critique, but they suggest that determining whether one's considered convictions favor Moore or the hedonist may not be so easy.

If, as Moore contends, "pleasure is *not* the sole good," then this fact "refutes half, or more than half, of the ethical theories which have ever been held" (195). In addition to rejecting hedonism, Moore repudiates the proposition that intrinsic value "is always in proportion to the quantity of any other *single* factor whatever" – for example, knowledge, virtue, or love. The reason is that "however valuable any one of these things may be, we may always add to the value of a whole which contains any one of them, not only by adding more of that one, but also *by adding something else instead*" (E 128). Thus, there is no single characteristic that always distinguishes a whole with greater intrinsic value from one with less.

3.2 The Greatest Goods and Evils

In his final defense of hedonism, Sidgwick appeals to the need to frame a unified and coherent account of ultimate good: "If we are not to systematize human activities by taking Universal Happiness as their common end, on what other principles are we to systematize them?" (Sidgwick, 1966: 406). In contrast, Moore denies the necessity of providing a theoretically unified account of the good, and he must have had Sidgwick in mind when he wrote that "we have no title whatever to assume that the truth of any subject-matter will display such symmetry as we desire to see" and admonished philosophers not "to search for 'unity' and 'system,' at the expense of truth" (270). Rather, Moore's view is simply that the things that are "intrinsically good or bad are many and various" (271). And the only way we can determine which things have intrinsic value and to what degree is by applying the method of isolation; that is, "by carefully distinguishing exactly what the thing is ... and then looking to see whether it has or has not the unique predicate 'good' in any of its various degrees" (271).

Once the method is clear, Moore thinks, then it becomes plain what the greatest goods are. Indeed, it is "so obvious, that it runs the risk of seeming to be a platitude" (237; cf. Russell, 1904: 331). Platitude or not, Moore's view occupies a distinctive place in the history of philosophy. The most valuable things are "the pleasures of human intercourse and the enjoyment of beautiful objects." No one has ever doubted, Moore writes, that they are good in themselves, nor is there anything else so worth having for its own sake (237). The categories of "personal affection and the appreciation of what is beautiful in Art or Nature ... include *all* the greatest, and *by far* the greatest, goods we can imagine" (237–8).

The proper appreciation of a beautiful object illustrates the complex, organic character of these wholes. It includes three elements. The first two are the cognition or consciousness of the object's beautiful qualities and an appropriate emotion toward those beautiful qualities. One element without the other is of slight value. Consider, Moore suggests, a person who listens to Beethoven's Fifth Symphony and feels the appropriate emotion but is not "aware of any of those melodic and harmonic relations, which are necessary to constitute the smallest beautiful elements in the Symphony" (241). Absent the cognitive element, the whole has little value. On the other hand, this element by itself is also insufficient. One must not only be aware of the object's qualities and know that they are beautiful; the person must also respond to them with the proper emotion.

The third element concerns knowledge of the existence of the beautiful object. Moore argues at length that "a true belief in the reality of [the beautiful] object greatly increases the value of many valuable wholes" (247). Although somewhat obscure, perhaps Moore's idea makes sense in some cases, but it leads him to believe that the emotionally appropriate contemplation of a natural scene is better than that of an equally beautiful painted landscape and, even more eccentrically, "that the world would be improved if we could substitute for the best works of representational art *real* objects equally beautiful" (243).

To define the beautiful as "that which produces certain effects upon our feelings" would be, Moore believes, to commit the naturalistic fallacy with respect to beauty. Moreover, it leads to an unacceptable subjectivism. For him, rather, beauty – like goodness – is an objective matter, and indeed there is a "consensus of opinion with regard to what is positively beautiful and what is positively ugly, and even with regard to great differences in degree of beauty." So Moore instead defines the beautiful as "that of which the admiring contemplation is good in itself" (247). Thus, "the question, whether [something] is *truly* beautiful or not, depends upon the *objective* question whether the whole in question is or is not truly good" (250). Furthermore, there is no single criterion of beauty. All that can be said is that "certain objects are beautiful, *because* they have certain characteristics, in the sense that they would not be beautiful *unless* they had them" (251). Moore thinks that his definition has the advantage of leaving only one unanalyzable predicate of value, namely, "good." Although "beautiful" is not identical to "good," it is defined by reference to it. To say that something is beautiful is not to say that it is itself good, but that it is a necessary element in something that is good (250). Donald Regan (2003: 674), for one, finds Moore's analysis "splendid," but other philosophers worry that defining the beautiful in terms of the good threatens to make trivial or vacuous Moore's claim that the admiring contemplation of beauty is of great intrinsic value (Ayer, 1982: 48; Baldwin, 1990: 130).

The pleasures of human affection, too, are organic wholes, involving the same essential constituents as valuable aesthetic enjoyments do: namely, "appropriate emotion, cognition of truly beautiful qualities, and true belief" (251). In contrast to aesthetic enjoyments, the object of personal affection "must be not only truly beautiful, but also truly good in a high degree." This goodness derives from the mental qualities of the person for whom the affection is felt. An appreciation of the other's mental qualities, though, is tied up with "an appreciation of the appropriate *corporeal* expression of the mental qualities in question ... whether by looks, by words, or by actions" (252). The admirable mental qualities, cognition of which is "essential to the value of human intercourse," include two things in particular: first, those "varieties of aesthetic appreciation" that form the first class of intrinsic goods; second, "the whole range of emotions, which are appropriate to persons" (253). And just as the value of those emotions depends on their appropriateness so, too, does the value of one's appreciation of another's emotions (253).

The goods involved in affectionate interpersonal relationships have a recursive quality; for instance, "the most valuable appreciation of persons appears to be that which consists in the appreciation of their appreciation of other persons" (252). As a result, it is unsurprising that Moore finds "that the study of what is valuable in human intercourse is a study of immense complexity" (253). Nevertheless, he believes that reflective judgment can correctly identify the basic goods of human interaction and any great differences in value among them. In particular, "the [most highly prized] emotions, of which the contemplation is essential to the greatest values, and which are also themselves appropriately excited by such contemplation," are those grouped "under the name of affection" (253).

In *Ethics* Moore maintains that "every intrinsic good must be a complex whole" containing "*both* some feeling and *also* some other form of consciousness" (E 129). In a subsequent essay, Moore wrote that "is intrinsically good" means "is an experience worth having for its own sake," which entails that nothing but an experience can be intrinsically good (Moore, 1962: 95). Although he later repudiated this as a mistake, Moore continued to affirm that no state of affairs can be good unless it entails that somebody is having some experience (Moore, 1952: 555, 618). Nevertheless, the value of a given state of affairs is neither equivalent nor proportional to the value of the experiences of the person or persons participating in it. The goodness of the whole is not an additive function of its goodness for them. This is true even if the valuable whole involves only one person. The appropriate appreciation of something beautiful is an objectively good state of affairs, but the reason why it is good is not, for Moore, that it is good for the person who is doing the appreciating. Perhaps the experience is indeed good for that person, making his or her life go better, but Moore does not say this, and even if true, in his eyes it is not the reason that the state of affairs is good. This is a noteworthy feature of Moore's value theory. It distinguishes it sharply from utilitarianism, which enjoins us to pursue happiness or well-being just because this is what is good for human beings (or other conscious creatures). For utilitarians, but not for Moore, the goodness of a state of affairs reduces to its goodness for individuals.

In principle, at least, hedonism ranks all states of affairs on a single scale according to their overall net pleasure or pain (E 7). By contrast, in Moore's view goodness and badness are not on a continuum. However, what Moore calls the great positive evils are comparable in one respect to the greatest positive goods because they are "organic unities of exactly the same nature. . . . That is to say, they are cognitions of some object, accompanied by some emotion" (256). Moore divides the great evils into three categories.[8]

The first category consists of the enjoyment or admiring contemplation of things that are evil or ugly. Cruelty and lasciviousness are Moore's examples. That they are great intrinsic evils is shown "by imagining the state of a man, whose mind is solely occupied by either of these passions, in their worst form" (257). The existence of a universe consisting solely of minds thus occupied would be worse than no universe at all (258; but cf. Smart, 1973: 25). These vicious states are, therefore, not only bad as means, but also bad in themselves. Few would doubt that cruelty is evil because it involves relishing the pain of others. But Moore also opines, less plausibly, that "the pleasures of lust . . . include both cognitions of organic sensations and perceptions of states of the body, of which the enjoyment is certainly an evil in itself" (258). As he sees it, lasciviousness not only includes an admiring contemplation of what is ugly but also, in its worst cases, involves enjoying the same state of mind in other people. More generally, either an increase in enjoyment or an increase in evilness or ugliness makes worse a cruel or lascivious state of affairs.

The second category of great evils – namely, hatred of what is good or beautiful – is similar to the first in its structure. Both differ, however, from the third category of great evils, which is consciousness of intense pain. It, too, is an organic unity involving both cognition and object, neither of which by itself has

---

[8] In *Principia* Moore uses "evil," whereas in *Ethics* he more typically employs "bad." To the modern ear, "evil" may carry a sense of being sinful, wicked, or blameworthy (although none of these connotations fit the third of Moore's three great positive evils).

"either merit or demerit." But it is "a less complex organic unity" than any other great evil or great good because there needn't be, in addition to a cognition, an emotion directed toward the object. Furthermore, the object here seems "absolutely simple" whereas in the other cases the object itself is always or almost always highly complex (261). More important, pleasure and pain are asymmetrical. Although consciousness of pleasure may have "some slight intrinsic value," it is not "a *great* good." Pain is a "far worse evil than pleasure is a good" (260). When combined with a good thing, pleasure adds to the goodness of the resulting whole greatly in excess of its own intrinsic value. By contrast, when combined with an evil state of mind, pain does not make the whole worse. Indeed, unless the pain is too great, "the whole thus formed is *always* better, *as a whole*, than if no pain had been there" (262). This claim underwrites the retributive view of punishment (discussed above at page 14), but even if one accepts Moore's general point, it must surely matter what the pain is and in what way it is a response to the evil mind. The world is not made better if someone who hates the natural beauty of the great outdoors suffers from chronic constipation.

Mixed goods are things that, though positively good as wholes, nevertheless contain something intrinsically evil or ugly as an essential element. Although intrinsically good, these wholes are not, in the terminology of *Ethics*, ultimately good or good for their own sake. Many virtuous dispositions – assuming they are intrinsically good rather than simply useful – are mixed goods. "Pity for the undeserved suffering of others, endurance of pain to ourselves, and a defiant hatred of evil dispositions in ourselves and in others" are admirable in themselves, but they are not, as we saw earlier, valuable on the whole (265–6). That is, it is not desirable that these evils exist in order that one can react virtuously to them. With the contemplation of imaginary evils, things are different. Responding in an emotionally appropriate way to the suffering of Lear or the vice of Iago is not only intrinsically good but also good on the whole (267).

3.3 The Value of the Virtues

Moore defines virtue as a "habitual disposition to perform certain actions, which generally produce the best possible results," arguing that we wouldn't consider a particular disposition virtuous if it were generally harmful (221). Not all useful dispositions, however, are virtues. Two further features distinguish them. First, virtues are dispositions it is particularly useful to praise or otherwise encourage; second, and related, they are dispositions leading to actions that people are frequently inclined to avoid. So far, this is an entirely consequentialist or instrumental approach to virtue, and determining which particular dispositions are virtues is an empirical question, the answer to which can vary with different states of society. However, Moore also believes that some virtues have intrinsic value or, more precisely, that the exercise of certain dispositions commonly regarded as virtues is intrinsically good (226). This is not an empirical issue.

Because of the good consequences that typically follow from the exercise of virtuous dispositions, we tend erroneously to rate their intrinsic value higher than we should (2005b: 148). But something is not good in itself just because it is a virtue. In fact, Moore thinks, most of the dispositions we consider virtues have no intrinsic value. He arrives at this conclusion by identifying three different mental states that are associated with virtuous dispositions and then considering the claims of each to be of intrinsic value.

(1)   Acting virtuously can be as habitual and mindless as pulling on our socks. That is, a person may habitually perform dutiful actions without ever thinking, when willing them, that they are duties or will have good results. "I, for instance," Moore writes, "am honest in the sense that I habitually refrain from any of the actions legally qualified as thieving, even where some other persons would be strongly tempted to commit them" (224). Such honesty is genuinely a virtue. Yet neither the exercise of this disposition nor the underlying disposition itself has the smallest intrinsic value. The majority of virtues are like this. Nor is this fact to be regretted because "a great economy of labour is effected when a useful action becomes habitual or instinctive" (225).

(2)   When a person habitually performs a certain duty, one of the motives may be love of some intrinsically good consequence (or hatred of some intrinsically bad consequence) that the person expects to produce (or hopes to prevent) by the action. And wherever a virtue consists in the disposition to be moved by such feelings, its exercise contains something that is good in itself – although the degree of goodness will vary with the precise nature of the motives and their object.

(3)   We call people conscientious if they always have rightness in mind when deliberating and if they act only when they are convinced their action is right (228). What are we to say of the virtue that consists in this disposition? The emotion "excited by rightness as such has some intrinsic value," Moore writes, and its presence may heighten the value of some wholes (228). But its intrinsic value is no greater than that of some other motives, in particular, love of things good in themselves, and he criticizes Kant for implying that conscientiousness is the sole good. Nor is conscientiousness "*more* useful than many other motives," let alone, as Kant thought, "*always* good as a means" (229). That's

because conscience does not invariably tell us the truth about what actions are right.

In the case of the virtues, as elsewhere, Moore believes that on reflection few people will dissent from his various judgments about what has intrinsic value or disvalue and to what degree. About this Moore was mistaken. Although his belief in the paramount value of "the love of beautiful things or of good persons" (272) was a central reason why the Bloomsbury literary group, which Moore was on the fringes of, so admired *Principia Ethica*, few professional philosophers have shared his opinion, and contemporary readers are likely to find it precious and idiosyncratic. For one thing, the great goods he identifies seem rather passive and contemplative, omitting the importance of creativity, achievement, and purposeful activity. This is not, of course, to deny the value of personal affection and aesthetic enjoyment, which utilitarians, for their part, will recommend reconceptualizing as components or aspects of human well-being.

Although the supreme value of the pleasures of human intercourse and the enjoyment of beautiful objects was, Moore thought, obvious, what was less obvious and what people have generally failed to recognize is

> the ultimate and fundamental truth of Moral Philosophy. That it is only for the sake of these things—in order that as much of them as possible may at some time exist—that any one can be justified in performing any public or private duty; that they are the *raison d'être* of virtue; that it is they—these complex wholes *themselves*, and not any constituent or characteristic of them—that form the rational ultimate end of human action and the sole criterion of social progress: these appear to be truths which have been generally overlooked. (238)

This statement is slightly inaccurate, however. It is not only for the sake of these great positive goods that we are justified in acting. We are also obligated to attenuate the evils Moore identifies because doing so makes the world better. This can be seen as a somewhat distinct avenue of duty because in his system goods and evils do not occupy the same continuum: To eliminate a Moorean evil is not necessarily to foster a Moorean good.

4 Right and Wrong

Although Moore's singular theory of value departs sharply from that of utilitarianism, his account of right and wrong is similar. Contemporary philosophers label "consequentialist" any theory that, like Moore's, shares the generic teleological structure of utilitarianism but not necessarily its account of good, and in recent decades they have increasingly made consequentialism an object of analysis in its own right.[9] This makes Moore's own insightful and sophisticated normative theory – long eclipsed by his contribution to metaethics and value theory – more relevant than ever.

Despite rejecting the hedonism of utilitarianism, Moore praises its theory of right. Utilitarianism is "fully justified," he affirms, in asserting that "right and wrong conduct must be judged by its results" and, more specifically, in "insisting that what is right must mean what produces the best possible results" (157; cf. 196). In *Ethics* he spends two chapters explaining and closely analyzing the normative structure of utilitarianism, making it clear that he agrees with that theory insofar as it declares that an action is right if and only if nothing else the agent could have done would have had better results; otherwise the action is wrong. Call this *the consequentialist principle*. According to it, an action could have bad consequences but yet be the right thing to do. This will be the case if the alternatives are worse. It could also happen that two actions have equally good outcomes. In that case, there is no single best and, hence, no uniquely right action. The agent acts rightly if he or she adopts either course.[10] As a result, although it is always our duty to act rightly, it is not true that if an action is right, then it is necessarily our duty to do that particular thing (E 15; cf. 148).

The consequentialist principle extends beyond the present to encompass actions that would have been right or wrong if they had been done in the past or would be right or wrong if they were to be done in the future. It gives us a "criterion, or test, or standard" of right and wrong and of what ought or ought not to be done that is "absolutely universal" (E 20–1). Properly understood, the principle goes even further. It affirms not only that right actions always do, as a matter of fact, bring about the best results, but also that they are right because and only because of this. In other words, the comparative goodness of their outcomes is the reason actions are right (or wrong) and not just a sign or an indicator that they are. Furthermore, the consequentialist principle holds true "in all conceivable circumstances and in any conceivable Universe" (E 26).

When we ask whether an action is our duty, we are asking whether it will have better results than anything else we could do. Moore acknowledges, however, that the word "duty" is commonly used in a more restricted sense to denote actions that have three additional characteristics: (1) they "excite moral approval" or their omission "excites moral disapproval," (2) "strong natural inclinations" disincline us to do them, and (3) their nonperformance "generally

---

[9] Moore never put a label on his normative system. Hastings Rashdall (1924) dubbed his own theory "ideal utilitarianism," a term sometimes applied to Moore, too. But that tag, rather misleading in any case, has fallen into disuse.

[10] The possibility of ties may seem a purely theoretical point, but it looms large in practice because of the difficulty of foreseeing and calculating future consequences.

entails consequences markedly disagreeable to *some one else*" (217–8). Many actions that maximize good (and which we are, therefore, morally required to do) lack one or more of these characteristics. This leaves us with a contrast between duty understood in a broad sense and duty understood in a narrow sense, the latter a subset of the former. Although the narrower sense may be truer to the everyday meaning of "duty," it is the broader sense that matters to Moore.

Nonconsequentialists characteristically contend that the rightness or wrongness of an action does not hang always or entirely on its outcome. Some of them do so because they believe that one's motive affects whether an action is right or wrong. By contrast, Moore strives to keep duty and motive separate. He grants, of course, that our everyday moral judgments do take account of motives. We rightly judge someone who does something with bad consequences but from a good motive differently from someone who does the same thing with a base or selfish motive. Yet, Moore argues, consideration of motives does not affect whether the action itself was right or wrong. Good motives do not make right an action that would otherwise be wrong, and bad motives do not make wrong an action that would otherwise be right (E 95).

Moore seeks to remove the temptation to think otherwise by explaining that, in addition to judgments of rightness and wrongness, we also make other moral judgments, judgments that do take account of motives. First, we assess motives themselves as good or bad. Good motives are those that tend to produce rightful conduct whereas bad motives are those likely to produce wrongful conduct. This assessment is compatible with acknowledging that sometimes bad motives can lead to right action and good motives to wrong. Second, motives are relevant to whether, and to what degree, an agent deserves moral praise or blame. When we say that an action deserves praise or blame, we imply, Moore says, that it is right to praise or blame the agent for it (E 97). This is a judgment, not about the rightness or wrongness of the original action, but rather about the rightness or wrongness of the further action we take in praising or blaming. One factor influencing the rightness or appropriateness of blame is whether blaming the agent will do some good by deterring her (or others) from doing similarly wrongful actions in the future. Obviously, if the agent acted wrongly from an otherwise admirable motive or from a motive unlikely to lead the person to act wrongly again, then blaming her will do little or no good.

Moore's third point is that some motives may be intrinsically good (and others intrinsically bad). This is consistent with the principle that right and wrong depend solely on an action's outcome, not on the motive from which it is done. The intrinsic value or disvalue of the agent's motives affects, not the rightness or wrongness of the action, but the goodness or badness of the overall state of affairs:

> If we suppose the same action to be done in one case from a good motive and in the other from a bad one, then, so far as the consequences of the action are concerned, the goodness of the whole state of things will be the same, while the presence of the good motive will mean the presence of an *additional* good in the one case which is absent in the other. (E 96)

But if this is so, can Moore consistently refuse to grant any weight to motives in the normative assessment of actions? Suppose that if Rebecca acts from a certain motive, then the overall state of affairs will be intrinsically better than it would otherwise have been. From this supposition it would seem to follow that the right course of action is for Rebecca to act from this particular motive. This argument assumes, of course, that it is within Rebecca's power to act from one motive rather than another. This assumption is open to doubt, and an unwillingness to grant it may perhaps explain why Moore believes that the presence or absence of certain motives may make the overall state of affairs better or worse without affecting the rightness or wrongness of what the agent does.

Moore overlooks a related consideration. Suppose that Rebecca's acting one way rather than another would somehow cause her or others to act from intrinsically good motives in the future, thus making the world better than it would otherwise have been. This fact should be relevant, on Moore's view, to the normative assessment of her action – in addition, of course, to any purely instrumental benefits of getting people to act from these motives.

4.1 Actual vs. Probable Results

According to the consequentialist principle, which Moore embraces, we are not merely permitted or encouraged, but morally required to act so as to bring about as much good as possible. As Moore stresses several times, when he refers to the results or consequences of an action, he has in mind the entire upshot of the action, that is, its overall outcome. He is concerned with whether, and to what extent, the world is better or worse because the agent has elected a given course of conduct. Thus, he takes into account whatever value, if any, the action has in itself as well as the goodness or badness of its effects (76; 1952: 560).

What matters to Moore are the actual consequences that an action has or will have (and that alternative actions would have had), rather than the consequences that were antecedently probable, that the agent had reason to expect, or that it was possible for one to foresee.[11] He was probably the first consequentialist to pose clearly the choice between an "actual-results" and a "probable-results" standard. Those who lean toward some form of probable-results consequential-ism do so because a conscientious agent could choose with the utmost care to act in the way that it was overwhelmingly reasonable to believe would produce the most good and, yet, because of unlikely or unforeseeable factors, this action turns out to have been suboptimal (E 99). Criticizing this unlucky agent for doing wrong seems harsh. As Moore acknowledges, it seems paradoxical to contend that the agent ought not to have chosen the course of conduct that at the time of decision he or she had every reason to think would be for the best – especially because we would want any agent, faced with an identical situation and the same information, to make the same choice. On the other hand, Moore finds it even more paradoxical to assert that an action was right when an alternative course of conduct would have made the world better (E 100–1; cf. 199–200).

Moore probably took an actual-results approach because of his commitment to ethical objectivity and his fear of making rightness a function of what people believe or even what it is reasonable for them to believe. On his behalf, one might argue that what consequentialists should care about is whether a contem-plated action will in fact maximize good, not just whether it is reasonable for a moral agent to believe that it will. Because the moral goal is to make the world as good as possible, it seems appropriate that achieving that goal – rather than adopting the means most likely to achieve it – should be the criterion of rightness, just as in principle the criterion of medical success is finding the treatment that is best for the patient, not simply the treatment that is likely to be best.

Moore makes his position more palatable by drawing on the distinction mentioned earlier between right and wrong, on the one hand, and what is blameworthy or praiseworthy, on the other. What we should say about the previously discussed careful but unlucky agent is not that her action was right but rather that she is free of blame. An action's wrongness does not entail the agent's blameworthiness. Nor, on the other hand, does rightness exempt an agent from criticism. Although an individual did what turned out to be right, the person may have acted recklessly or with wicked intention. But what are we to say to an agent beforehand, when the question of what one ought to do is still open? Moore's answer is that we can be justified in saying that an agent

---

[11] Because in Moore's view an action is wrong if and only if it is possible for the agent to do something better, one might argue that if an action does not occur to an agent, then it is impossible for him to do it, thus narrowing the gap between actual-results and probable-results consequentialism. But Moore rejects this maneuver (200).

absolutely ought to choose the action that (as far as one can see) will be the best, even though it may really be true (as one will learn later) that she ought not to have chosen that particular action (E 101).

In line with this, some consequentialists distinguish between objective rightness and the action it would have been reasonable or subjectively right for the agent to perform. Moore once came close to acknowledging such a distinction when he commented "that, in one sense, an action is right if, and only if, it actually does promote the general good as much as possible and that, in another sense, it is right if, and only if, the agent has reason to think that it will," but he never explicitly endorsed this suggestion or advocated dividing rightness into two kinds (1907–8: 447). His view, rather, is that we can be justified in saying that the agent ought to choose the action that appears best because we can be justified in saying something that we do not know for certain to be true, such as "x is the morally required course of action," if there is a strong probability that it is true (E 101). However, this statement faces the complication that in some situations of uncertainty we don't want the agent to choose the action that, were it to succeed, would have the best result. Rather, we want the agent to choose the action with the greatest expected value (the expected value of an action being the sum of the goodness or badness of its possible effects multiplied by their probabilities) even if this action is certain not to produce the best possible outcome. Sometimes the course of action that could produce the most good is too risky to take (for examples, see Zimmerman, 2008: 17–8; Parfit, 2011–7, I: 159–60).

Perhaps actual-results consequentialists like Moore can accommodate this point and endorse a policy of acting so as to maximize expected value (but see Andrić, 2013). Still, their standard of right faces some problems. For one thing, comparing the actual results of what we did with what the actual results would have been, had we done something else instead, becomes problematic if determinism is false. In a nondeterministic world, the notion of "what the actual consequences of an alternative action would have been" is indeterminate. This is not indeterminacy in what we can know, but in the way things are. There is simply no fact of the matter as to what would have happened. And even if the world is fully deterministic, our actions have effects that extend indefinitely into the future with repercussions we cannot even begin to guess at. True, we tend to assume that we can safely ignore the distant effects of our actions and that the "consequences of our action in a further future" will not "reverse the balance of good that is probable in the future we can foresee" (202). This assumption seems plausible, but has not yet been shown to be true (203, 230). Still, despite these difficulties, one might urge on Moore's behalf that an actual-results criterion of right provides an ideal against which we can sometimes judge even perfectly responsible conduct to have failed (Smith, 2006: 447).

4.2 The Case for Consequentialism

In support of their normative theory, utilitarians frequently appeal to the fact that we care deeply about human well-being and value happiness so highly. If morality is not about promoting the well-being or happiness of individuals, they ask, then what could it plausibly be about? Moore's consequentialism rests on no analogous appeal to the value we place on personal affection or aesthetic enjoyment. Indeed, in *Principia* Moore discusses these great goods only in the final chapter – that is, only after he has already advanced his account of right and wrong and said everything he has to say about ethical conduct. Likewise in *Ethics* he upholds the consequentialist standard of right and wrong without positively identifying the things that are intrinsically good or bad.

Although Moore's defense of consequentialism relies on no specific value claims, he believes that there is a deep tie between "good" and "ought." For something to be intrinsically good, he believes, just is for it to be something that ought to be preferred to nothing at all, and for something to be intrinsically better than something else just is for the first thing to be something that ought to be preferred to the second (E 32). "It would always be wrong," he writes, "to prefer a *worse* set of total consequences to a *better*" (E 83). We ought not only to prefer the better state of affairs, but also try to bring it about: "it must always be the duty of any being who had to choose between two actions, one of which he *knew* would have *better* total effects than the other, to choose the former" (E 87). In an early series of lectures, Moore writes that to describe something as good is to say that it ought to be, and he urges his listeners to accept the principle that "you ought always to do that which is a means to what ought to be" (1991: 118). Unless we accept this principle, he proclaims, we cannot give a reason for our conduct – an assertion that carries over into *Principia Ethica*: "The only possible reason that can justify any action is that by it the greatest possible amount of what is good absolutely should be realised" (153). This is "the one supreme rule of Practical Ethics" (1903b: 122).

Principia maintains that our ethical terminology itself reflects this link between the rightness of an action and the comparative, net goodness of its outcome. This makes consequentialism, in effect, a definitional truth. Consider these examples:

The assertions "This action is right" or "is my duty" are equivalent to the assertion that the total results of the action in question will be the best possible. (47)

In asserting that the action is *the* best thing to do, we assert that it together with its consequences presents a greater sum of intrinsic value than any possible alternative. (76)

The assertion "I am morally bound to perform this action" is identical with the assertion "This action will produce the greatest amount of good in the Universe." (197)

Our "duty," therefore, can only be defined as that action, which will cause more good to exist in the Universe than any possible alternative. And what is "right" or "morally permissible" only differs from this, as what will *not* cause *less* good than any possible alternative. (198)

Unfortunately for Moore, his open-question argument can be turned against these supposed definitional equivalences. There is, after all, no absurdity in saying "I know this action would have the best possible results, but I still want to know whether it is morally required of me." Moore came to accept this rejoinder, later writing that Bertrand Russell had persuaded him that it could hardly be true "to say that 'This is what I ought to do' is merely a shorter way of saying 'The Universe will be a better Universe if I do this than if I were to do instead anything else which I could do'" (1952: 558).

Moore nevertheless persisted in believing that "the conceptions 'intrinsically better' and 'intrinsically worse' are connected in a perfectly precise manner with the conceptions 'right' and 'wrong'" (E 32). And *Ethics* expressly reaffirms the proposition that an action is right only if no action, which the agent could have done instead, would have had intrinsically better results, and wrong only if some alternative action would have had better results (E 30). Contrary to what *Principia* implied, this "very important proposition," Moore now writes, is no tautology. Nevertheless, the proposition that A has greater intrinsic value than B and the proposition that it is my duty to choose A rather than B always have the same truth value: "whenever the one is true, the other is certainly also true" (E 30). Thus, although Moore abandoned the contention that "This is what I ought to do" is identical in meaning to "The Universe will be a better Universe if I do this than if I were to do instead anything else," he saw the two as logically equivalent, with each proposition following from the other (1952: 599).

"X is a cube" and "X is a cube and X has twelve edges" is a nonethical example of two propositions that are logically equivalent without being identical in meaning; so is "The sun is larger than the moon" and "If any one were to believe that the sun is larger than the moon he would be right" (1952: 600–1). Likewise, for Moore, "I ought to do this action" follows from the proposition that "the subsequent effects of this action would be intrinsically better than those of anything else that I could do instead." The converse also holds: from "I ought to do this" it follows that "the subsequent effects of this act would be intrinsically better." There is, in other words, "a necessary and *reciprocal* connection" between these two notions (1952: 563).

Why is this? Moore's answer is simply that it is self-evident. Thus, *Ethics* asserts as "self-evident" the principle "that it must always be the duty of any being who had to choose between two actions, one of which he *knew* would have *better* total effects than the other, to choose the former" (E 87) and later reiterates that it is "quite self-evident that it must always be our duty to do what will produce the best effects *upon the whole*" (E 121).

As Moore sees it, those who disagree believe, to the contrary, that certain kinds of actions are always absolutely right and that certain rules should never be broken "*whatever* the consequences might be" (E 91). But those who think this, he argues, typically assume that acting in the required way will not in fact have worse consequences than would acting otherwise. They do not squarely consider whether breaking a rule they consider absolute would be wrong if doing so were to bring about the best possible outcome. However, if they were to reflect on the extreme improbability that any specific kind of action will absolutely always and in all circumstances produce the best possible results, then most people would, Moore thinks, abandon the view that some actions ought absolutely always to be performed regardless of the consequences (E 93).

Still, Moore concedes, some people may continue to affirm that certain actions ought absolutely always to be done "*whatever* the consequences may be, and even, therefore, if the total consequences are not the best possible" (E 93). These people thus believe that right and wrong depend "merely on the *intrinsic nature* of the action" (E 117), and they hold that we are unconditionally to avoid certain kinds of actions. This deontological stance, of course, directly contradicts Moore's consequentialism. However, if someone adopts it, clearly understanding its meaning and implications, then there is, Moore believes, "no way of refuting it except by appealing to the self-evidence" of the principle that "if we *knew* that the effect of a given action really would be to make the world, as a whole, *worse* than it would have been if we had acted differently, it would certainly be wrong for us to do that action" (E 93–4).

Satisfied with this appeal to self-evidence, Moore confidently repudiates the absolutist position that certain things are right or wrong "whatever the conse-quences." His resolute rejection of this position may indeed be warranted, and he is probably right that many people who think they hold it would abandon it on fuller reflection. Faced with the standard counterexamples – telling a lie to throw a murderer off the trail or preventing World War II by assassinating Hitler in 1938 – and thinking these through, many would-be absolutists might well give up their categorical adherence to certain moral rules. However, Moore's defense of the consequentialist principle illicitly benefits from lumping together distinct nonconsequentialist positions. The extreme "whatever the consequences" position is far from the most plausible rival to Moore's principle that whether an action is right or wrong depends entirely on its outcome. The "whatever the consequences" stance entails that an action can be right even if its consequences are not the best possible. But someone can believe the latter without believing that consequences are totally irrelevant to rightness and wrongness. Denying, as the moderate nonconsequentialist does, that consequences are the whole story, morally speaking, does not entail that they play no role at all.

Both moderate and extreme nonconsequentialists justify their moral rules, the following of which may sometimes conflict with the consequentialist principle, by appeal to intuition. Moore thinks, to the contrary, that "it is plain that no moral law is self-evident" (198). Moore, of course, believes that the consequentialist principle is self-evident as is the truth or falsity of certain propositions about the value of various things or states of affairs. What he rejects is "the Intuitional view of ethics" or what might be called intuitionism at the normative level: namely, the view that some rules requiring or forbidding reasonably specific types of human conduct are intuitively certain (198).

Moore's use of the terms *self-evident* and *intuition* requires some clarification. To call a proposition "self-evident" means, Moore writes, "that the proposition so called is evident or true, *by itself* alone" (193). It is not an inference from some other proposition. Nor does its truth rest on epistemic conviction. This is an important point. That a proposition appears certain to us, Moore states emphatically, is not the reason it is true. Its appearing evident to us may be the cause of our asserting it and thus, in a sense, the reason we think and say that it is true. It may even be a reason we ought to believe it or to affirm its truth. But a proposition is not self-evident, Moore contends, just because we cannot think otherwise. Our conviction of its truth is neither proof nor evidence. A "logical reason" is a reason why a proposition must be true, not why we hold it to be true, and in this sense a self-evident proposition has no reason: There are, that is to say, no reasons that establish its truth (193–4). If our conviction of its truth were the reason a proposition is true, then it would not be self-evident.

In line with this, Moore writes that when he refers to a proposition as an "intuition," he is merely asserting that it is incapable of proof or disproof (36). The original index to *Principia*, though, divides "intuition" into two entries: "proposition incapable of proof" and "in a psychological sense" (276). This reflects an important distinction for Moore. On the one hand, one can describe or refer to a self-evident proposition as an "intuition" in the sense of being something knowable only by direct apprehension (and the truth of which cannot be established by evidence and reason). On the other hand, "intuition" can be used to designate someone's psychological conviction – his or her epistemic sense – that a proposition must be true, leaving it open whether the proposition really is either true or self-evident. Moore respects this distinction. For example, he writes that when he denies that "pleasure is the only good," his intuition of its falsehood is his reason for believing it untrue, but his denial is not based on that intuition: "There is no proper evidence or reason of its falsehood except itself alone. It is untrue, because it is untrue, and there is no other reason" (194). Furthermore, there is no necessary connection between the two senses of intuition. In particular, calling something an intuition in the first sense (a truth incapable of proof) implies nothing whatsoever about "the manner or origin of our cognition of [it]." To the contrary, Moore specifically asserts "that in every way that it is possible to cognise a true proposition, it is also possible to cognise a false one" (36).

Thus, when Moore opposes what he calls intuitionism by asserting that no moral rules are self-evident, he is maintaining that no propositions concerning the rightness or wrongness of specific types of actions are simply true in themselves. To be sure, we often judge the rightness or wrongness of actions immediately, and we frequently feel intuitively certain of our duty. But these psychological facts do not entail that these judgments are true, still less that their truth lies beyond argument or evidence. On Moore's mature view, the consequentialist principle itself is an intuition in the sense of being a self-evidently true proposition that is incapable of proof. But in making results the criterion of right and wrong, the principle entails that the truth of any specific normative judgment is not self-evident but rather must be "confirmed or refuted by an investigation of causes and effects" (198). This underscores a point fundamental to the entire utilitarian or consequentialist tradition. To acknowledge certain moral rules as self-evident would be to accept them as valid independently of any external standard of assessment and, a fortiori, as valid independently of the consequentialist standard.

Critics frequently argue that, in certain sets of circumstances, utilitarian or other consequentialist theories can require actions that we know intuitively to be wrong. Because these critics commonly leave their own metaethical commitments unstated, the precise meaning of "intuitive" is unclear. By describing a moral judgment as an "intuition," they may mean only that they firmly believe it or that they find it immediately certain in a psychological sense – and not that it is self-evident in Moore's sense. Thus, their appeal to "intuition" does not necessarily challenge, let alone disprove, his thesis that there are no self-evident moral rules, and consequentialists, for their part, regularly take steps to try to disarm the intuitive moral judgments of their critics or show how a consequentialist approach can accommodate them. Still, at the present stage of normative debate, consequentialists can hardly rest as content as Moore does with a stark and unvarnished appeal to self-evidence – an appeal that is unlikely to persuade those not already inclined to the consequentialist cause.

4.3 The Objectivity of Right and Wrong

Living up to the consequentialist normative principle can be problematic because we rarely, if ever, know all the possible outcomes of our actions or their likelihoods, let alone those of the alternative actions we could have performed. Accurately measuring and comparing the goodness of those outcomes are also difficult – not least because doing so may involve debatable value judgments. Nevertheless, like other consequentialists Moore maintains that in principle questions of right and wrong have objective answers, however hard they may be to obtain in practice. Further, and more specifically, his consequentialism implies that a particular action – say, Brutus's stabbing Caesar – cannot be both right and wrong, either at the same time or at different times. At any particular time, Moore contends, this action must be either right or wrong, and whichever it is, that it was right (or wrong) at that time will never change (E 40).

In *Ethics* and elsewhere Moore argues at length against theories that deny this proposition and thus reject what he sees as the objectivity of moral judgments.[12] If these theories were correct, then it would follow – in contradiction to Moore's consequentialism – that "there can be no characteristic which *always* belongs to right actions, and *never* to wrong ones" (E 42). Although he believes that it is self-evident that no voluntary action can be both right and wrong, this judgment cannot be proved. "Like all ultimate questions, it is incapable of strict proof either way" (E 43). However, Moore believes that it is possible to marshal independent arguments against the most common theories that entail or imply that actions can be both right and wrong, and this is what he endeavors to do. The theories he has in mind treat moral obligation as "merely a psychological idea" by making right and wrong a function of the mental attitudes of some person or set of persons (2005b: 157; E 116).

One influential theory of this sort – call it "private subjectivism" – maintains that when one asserts an action to be right or wrong, one is asserting merely that

---

[12] Or, rather, what Moore sees as the objectivity of moral judgments in one important sense of objectivity. The subjectivist and attitudinal theories he discusses do not undercut the objectivity of moral judgments in every sense (1907–8: 451; 1993a: 282–5).

one has some particular feeling or attitude toward the action in question. It might be, Moore observes, that whenever one judges an action right, then one has some feeling toward that action; it might even be that one makes such a judgment only because one has a certain feeling. But private subjectivism goes beyond this. It holds that judgments about right or wrong are simply judgments about one's own feelings (whatever the relevant feelings are taken to be). In this view, "the word 'wrong' in my mouth means something entirely different from what it does in yours; just as the word 'I' in my mouth stands for an entirely different person from what it does in yours" (2005b: 152).

Although Moore says he is unaware of any positive arguments for private subjectivism (2005b: 151), he takes it to be a common view – so common that many people have difficulty seeing how "right" and "wrong" could possibly mean anything else (E 43). However, a problem arises, he thinks, from the fact that sometimes two different people have opposite feelings toward the same action. When this happens, private subjectivism implies that there is no difference in moral opinion between them. Moore maintains that this fact constitutes an "absolutely fatal objection" to private subjectivism:

> If, when one man says, "This action is right," and another answers, "No, it is not right," each of them is always merely making an assertion about *his own* feelings, it plainly follows that there is never really any difference of opinion between them: the one of them is never really contradicting what the other is asserting. . . . [But] it is surely plain matter of fact that when I assert an action to be wrong, and another man asserts it to be right, there sometimes is a real difference of opinion between us: he is sometimes denying the very thing which I am asserting. (E 50–1)

Decades later Charles Stevenson defended private subjectivism against Moore's attack. When A says "X is right" and B says "X is not right," they need not be differing in their beliefs about X, as Moore thinks, but rather in the attitudes they are expressing toward X (Stevenson, 1952: 82). What Moore takes to be a case of differing moral opinions may only be a case of conflicting attitudes. If so, then private subjectivism would not contradict a "plain matter of fact," as Moore alleges, because people could differ in moral matters without holding logically incompatible opinions.

In defense of Moore, one might argue that "X is right" contradicts "X is not right" in a way that "I approve of X" when said by one person does not contradict "I disapprove of X" when said by another (White, 1969: 131). In reply to Stevenson, however, Moore conceded that his original argument may have been inconclusive, but he did not revise his opinion of private subjectivism. Although he acknowledged that avowing that Brutus was right to stab Caesar suggests or implies that one approves of Brutus's doing so, Moore nevertheless maintains that to assert that the action is right is not to assert that one approves of it, nor is one's approval entailed by what one does assert (1952: 540–4, 547). And he balked at the idea, implicit in Stevenson's position, that "right" means something different when used by different speakers or by the same speaker at different times (1952: 552).

Moore consistently rejected private subjectivism, but he was unsure what to make of the more radical noncognitivism suggested by some of Stevenson's remarks. This more radical position holds that when one asserts, for example, that Brutus acted wrongly in stabbing Caesar, one is asserting nothing that is either true or false – that is, that the speaker's words have no cognitive meaning or propositional content. One is not saying (as private subjectivism contends), "I disapprove of Brutus's action," which is a proposition with truth value. Rather, one is simply expressing a negative attitude toward the action and perhaps also trying to get others to share one's disapproval of it. This noncognitivist stance is incompatible with Moore's long-standing view that right and wrong refer to objective features of the world independent of the agent. But in his response to Stevenson, Moore vacillated, writing that he had both some inclination to accept noncognitivism and some inclination not to accept it: "And, if you ask me to which of these incompatible views I have the *stronger* inclination, I can only answer that I simply do not know. . . . I think this is at least an honest statement of my present attitude" (1952: 545).[13] Throughout his career, Moore resisted subjectivism in ethics, but as this passage indicates, he never came fully to grips with noncognitivism, the influence of which was growing just as he was retiring from philosophy.

In *Ethics* Moore goes on, in patient detail, to debunk several other attitudinal theories of ethics in addition to private subjectivism, including the thesis that moral judgments are assertions about what most people in one's society feel and the thesis that when one judges an action to be right (or wrong), one is merely asserting that one believes that the action is right (or wrong). As he explains, these views are vulnerable to additional objections beyond those lodged against private subjectivism. Moore also criticizes the theory that right and wrong are determined by what God commands or forbids us to do. Even if God exists and commands all that is right and only what is right (and forbids all that is wrong and only what is wrong), this is not what we mean when calling something right

---

[13] However, in the same essay Moore describes noncognitivism as "paradoxical," and immediately after saying for the second time that he does not know which way he is more inclined, he gives a reason for thinking noncognitivism false (1952: 554). A. C. Ewing later reported that Moore continued to cleave to his old view and in fact said that "he could not imagine whatever in the world had induced him to say that he was almost equally inclined to hold the other view" (Ewing, 1962: 251).

(or wrong). Furthermore, the theory entails "that there is absolutely *no* class of actions of which we can say that it always *would*, in any conceivable Universe, be right or wrong." That's because it is possible that God does not exist, in which case nothing would be right or wrong (E 79). Moore's critique of these various attitudinal theories is compelling. Indeed, his arguments are so widespread and influential that they now seem quite familiar.[14]

4.4 The Challenge of Egoism

Subjectivist or attitudinal theories challenge a wide range of ethical views. So does egoism, understood as the thesis that one ought only to pursue one's own interests. Indeed, it stands opposed to any ethical theory that obliges us sometimes to put other considerations ahead of self-interest. But because egoism is consequentialist in structure, it confronts Moore's universalistic consequentialism head-on. This is because the action with the best outcome overall may not be best for the agent herself. Moore distinguishes two versions of egoism. One asserts "that it can never be the duty of any agent to sacrifice his good to the general good." A stronger version holds that "it must *always* be an agent's positive duty to do what is best for *himself*" even if this does not have the best possible consequences overall (E 119). Both versions contradict the consequentialist principle.

In *Principia* Moore's critique of egoism focuses on what is meant by the phrase "my own good" or by saying that something is "good for me." These locutions, he thinks, can only mean "that the thing I get is good, or that my possessing it is good" (150). When I describe a thing as "my own good," Moore writes, "all that I can mean is that something which will be exclusively mine, as my own pleasure is mine ... is also *good absolutely*" (150). The good of it does not belong to me; it is not private. "'My own good,'" he argues, "only denotes some event affecting me, which is good absolutely and objectively; it is the thing, and not its goodness, which is *mine*." Thus, as Moore sees it, "everything must be either 'a part of universal good' or else not good at all; there is no third alternative conception 'good for me'" (219).

If someone says that his actions are justified because they promote his own good, "he must mean that this is the greatest possible amount of Universal Good which he can realise" (153). For the only reason I can have for aiming at "my own good," Moore believes, is that what I am aiming at is good objectively or absolutely. "But if it is *good absolutely* that I should have it, then everyone else has as much reason for aiming at *my* having it, as I have myself" (150). Egoism

---

[14] Ross probably spoke for many when he wrote that Moore's "line of argument seems to me unanswerable" (1930: 82).

thus entails, Moore argues, that each person's good is the sole good – that is, "that a number of different things are *each* of them the only good thing there is" – which is a contradiction. He concludes that "no more complete and thorough refutation of any theory could be desired" (151). This refutation, Moore thinks, vindicates the principle that "self-sacrifice may be a real duty; just as the sacrifice of any single good, whether affecting ourselves or others, may be necessary in order to obtain a better total result" (219). If something is good, then "everyone else has an equal reason to pursue it, so far as they are able and so far as it does not exclude their attainment of other more valuable parts of Universal Good" (153; cf. Russell, 1910: 47, and Kagan, 1989: 61).

Although Moore neglects to mention it, his argument derives from his teacher Henry Sidgwick. Sidgwick had written that if the egoist

> puts forward, implicitly or explicitly, the proposition that his happiness or pleasure is Good, not only *for him* but from the point of view of the Universe . . . it then becomes relevant to point out to him that *his* happiness cannot be a more important part of Good, taken universally, than the happiness of any other person. (Sidgwick, 1966: 420–1)

Yet Sidgwick thought that an avenue of escape was open to the egoist. The egoist could avoid the above conclusion by simply declining to affirm "that his own greatest happiness is not merely the ultimate rational end for himself, but a part of Universal Good" (Sidgwick, 1966: 497). In other words, "it cannot be proved that the difference between [the egoist's] own happiness and another's happiness is not *for him* all-important" (Sidgwick, 1966: 420).

To this Moore vigorously objects:

> That a thing should be an ultimate rational end means, then, that it is truly good in itself; and that it is truly good in itself means that it is part of Universal Good. Can we assign any meaning to that qualification "for himself," which will make it cease to be part of Universal Good? The thing is impossible: for the Egoist's happiness must *either* be good in itself, and so a part of Universal Good, *or else* it cannot be good in itself at all: there is no escaping this dilemma. And if it is not good at all, what reason can he have for aiming at it? How can it be a rational end for him? (151)

Egoism, Moore is arguing, inevitably entails that the agent's own happiness is objectively good; otherwise, the theory would provide the agent with no reason for acting. If so, then there is no dodging the original contradiction facing egoism – namely, in holding that each person ought to aim only at his or her own good, it implies that each and every person's good is the only objective good.

Two suppositions, which we have brushed up against before, underlie Moore's reasoning. The first is his belief that goodness is an objective property of things or states of affairs and not something that is relative to the agent. If a state of affairs is good, then it is good, period, and this is so regardless of one's particular perspective or point of view. Indeed, contrary to Sidgwick, he thought that the very idea of a thing being "good for me" but not good per se or good absolutely makes no sense.[15] The second supposition is Moore's belief that the only reason one can have for acting, the only rational end, is to achieve as much good as can be achieved: "the only possible reason that can justify any action is that by it the greatest possible amount of what is good absolutely should be realised" (153). This belief explains why Moore writes "sufficient reason" rather than "sufficient moral reason" when he asserts that "the fact that an action is really to my interest can never be a sufficient reason for doing it" (219). Whereas for Sidgwick the most profound problem of ethics is the conflict between rational egoism and rational benevolence (Sidgwick, 1966: 386 n), Moore maintains that "to say that I have to choose between my own good and that of *all* is a false antithesis" (155). The only rational question is how to choose between myself and others so as to bring about as much good as possible.

Moore evidently came to have some doubts about *Principia*'s rebuttal of egoism for when he discussed egoism in *Ethics*, he no longer maintained that it is self-contradictory. Rather, he writes that no argument for or against egoism is decisive and that it would be impossible to prove that someone is mistaken who "after clearly considering the question, comes to the conclusion that he can never be under any obligation to sacrifice his own good to the general good" (E 120). On the other hand, however, it would be equally impossible for this person to demonstrate that he was not mistaken. Moore continues: "For my part, it seems to me quite self-evident that he is mistaken. It seems to me quite self-evident that it must always be our duty to do what will produce the best effects *upon the whole*, no matter how bad the effects upon ourselves may be and no matter how much good we ourselves may lose by it" (E 121). On the strength of this, Moore concludes that egoism may safely be rejected.

---

[15] Rashdall (1924: I, 79n) and Mackie (1976: 322–3), among others, challenge this. Some contemporary philosophers go to the opposite extreme from Moore, contending that it makes no sense to say that a state of affairs can be just plain good (or bad or better than another) – that is, that nothing can be good *simpliciter* as opposed to being good (or bad or better) for someone or some purpose or relative to some point of view (e.g., Thomson, 2001: 17–9).

5 Ethics in Practice

According to the consequentialist principle, which Moore endorses unequivocally, an action is right if and only if no other action available to the agent would bring about more good. Determining whether an action meets this standard would, as we have seen, require foreseeing and comparing through an indefinite future the effects of all the actions the agent could have performed in the given circumstances. Our causal knowledge is, to say the least, far too incomplete for this. As a result, we can never be sure that a particular action will produce the greatest value possible (198–9).

Nevertheless, we may be able to show that of the limited set of actions likely to occur to anyone, one will probably produce more good in the foreseeable future. This is the "humbler task" of practical ethics (199). More specifically, practical ethics asks whether we can "lay down any general rules to the effect that one among a few alternative actions will generally produce a greater total of good in the immediate future" (203–4). And the answer to this question is yes. "It seems possible," Moore writes, "to establish as much as this in defence of most of the rules most universally recognised by Common Sense" (205).

5.1 Moral Rules

Consequentialists generally agree that one should recommend a rule to others and follow it oneself if and only if better results generally come from people acting in accord with the rule than from their following some other rule or no rule at all. And this is what Moore hopes to establish with regard to the most basic rules of everyday morality: "If . . . we give the name of 'duty' to actions which *generally* produce better total results in the near future," he writes, then we can "prove that a few of the commonest rules of duty are true" (230).

5.1.1 The Universal Core of Ordinary Morality

Although it occupies only a page of *Principia Ethica*, Moore's defense of the commonsense prohibition of murder is his most thorough discussion of any specific normative rule. The disutility of murder (and thus the utility of a moral rule against it) rests on two things. First, there are "the immediate evils which murder generally produces" (206). Moore leaves these unelaborated, but presumably they include the loss of the goods that the deceased would have created or participated in had he or she lived, and the sorrow, distress, and inconvenience that his or her death causes other people.

Second, and this is the point Moore stresses, if murder were a common practice, then the insecurity it would breed – given that people strongly desire to continue living – would absorb time and effort that might be spent to better purpose, hindering people "from devoting their energy to the attainment of positive goods" (206). Moore does not mean that murder is wrong because it thwarts people's desire to live. Rather, he contends that because people do in fact strongly desire to live, if murder were permitted, then the threat of it would divert them from pursuing morally valuable aims. Thus, "it is generally wrong for any single person to commit murder" (206).

One might object that the fact if murder were a common practice, then it would cause insecurity gives us a reason only for thinking that it would be bad for murder to be a common practice. It does not show that an isolated murder would be wrong or that a rule banning murder altogether is necessary. Moore, however, has probably understated his case. Murder need not be a common practice before human beings begin to feel insecure. A distant murder or two or a certain probability of murder may be all that is needed to induce people to take steps to make themselves feel more secure, thus diverting them from the pursuit of more valuable goods. Those of us fortunate enough to feel generally safe from murder and, thus, able to attend to other things should bear in mind that we do so thanks in part to a criminal justice system that represents a social expenditure of money, time, and energy that might otherwise be directed toward things that are intrinsically worthwhile.

Moore assumes that a society must either tolerate murder or ban it and that if murder is not proscribed, then it will be widespread. These assumptions simplify the situation in some significant ways. For instance, our society tolerates, morally and legally, certain direct killings and overlooks altogether some failures to sustain the lives of others. It ranks those homicides it forbids according to their perceived degree of wrongfulness and punishes killers in line with this. Consequentialists do not need simply to decide whether to permit murder (indeed, the very notion of a legal or morally permissible "murder" borders on the oxymoronic). Rather, the significant task for them is to determine when, under what circumstances, and to what extent killing people (as well as letting them die) is not to be tolerated and thus to determine, among other things, which homicides, of whom, and under what circumstances are to be condemned as murders.

On any plausible theory of the good, murder will almost always produce more direct evil than it will good. But Moore anchors the case against murder on the disvalue of its indirect effects: Murder and the threat of murder interfere with the ability of people to secure important goods. Like considerations, Moore argues, also support most of the rules "most universally enforced by legal sanctions" (protection of property is his example) and some of the rules "most commonly recognised by Common Sense" (he mentions industry, temperance, and the keeping of promises). Because people have an "intense desire for property of some sort," a desire that seems to be universal, the rules that protect property "serve greatly to facilitate the best possible expenditure of energy." Likewise, industry, temperance, and promise keeping greatly assist our acquiring those things that are necessary for "the further attainment of any great positive goods" (206–7).

These rules display two significant characteristics. First, "in any known state of society, a *general* observance of them *would* be good as a means." Their utility reflects desires that are universal and strong (207). Observing these rules, then, is an indispensable prerequisite for obtaining important moral goods, and in any case, Moore adds, doing so never makes society worse off than nonobservance would. Again, Moore is not arguing that the core rules of morality, which facilitate the satisfaction of elementary desires and the securing of life's necessities, are valuable because the desires they satisfy are valuable. Rather, they are good purely as means, valuable only because by addressing those desires they remove obstacles to our attaining those things that truly are intrinsically good.

Second, these rules can be defended independently of a correct view about what is intrinsically good. Because they are essential for the preservation of civilized society, they are, in turn, "necessary for the existence, in any great degree, of anything which may be held to be good in itself" (207; cf. 47). Moore does not foreclose in principle justifying certain moral rules by showing their direct tendency to produce what is good in itself or prevent what is bad in itself (209, 214). But he is skeptical of this approach, reminding us that "a correct judgment of what things are good or bad in themselves . . . has never yet been offered by ethical writers" (230; cf. 208). Yet, in the next chapter of *Principia*, Moore presents his own account of the most important goods and evils, which, as we have seen, he takes to be uncontroversial. Rather than appealing to this, however, he prefers instead to justify the core rules of everyday morality by what he calls "the ordinary method, which tries to shew in them a tendency to that preservation of society, which is itself a mere means" (214). This parsimoniousness of method is appealing, avoiding as it does reliance on possibly contestable judgments of goodness.

5.1.2 Rules Resting on Contingent Circumstances

As we have just seen, Moore believes that in any society the general observance of certain basic moral rules would be good. He recognizes, however, that this is not true of all the rules of commonsense morality. Arguments in favor of these other rules can prove their utility only "so long as certain conditions, which may alter, remain the same: it cannot be claimed ... that they would be generally good as a means in every state of society" (207).

For example, vindicating those "rules comprehended under the name of Chastity" presupposes the "existence of such sentiments as conjugal jealousy and paternal affection." In societies where these sentiments are sufficiently strong and widespread, consequentialists can uphold the rules in question. But we err if we assume "the necessary existence of such sentiments" (208). To the contrary, Moore writes, one can easily imagine a civilized society without them. To exonerate traditional sexual morality in such a society, consequentialist analysis would have to establish that violating these rules would produce "evil effects, other than those due to the assumed tendency of such violation to disintegrate society," which in turn would require "a correct view of what is good and bad in itself" (208).[16] A distinction therefore needs to be drawn between those rules the utility of which rests on circumstances "more or less likely to alter" and those whose "utility seems certain under all possible conditions" (208).

Although the commonsense moral rules "in the society in which we live" are often defended as if "they were all equally and universally right and good," these rules are, in fact, "of very different orders" (209). Some depend on conditions that are permanent and ineradicable, but even these often owe their more obvious utilities to conditions that "cannot be taken to be necessary except over longer or shorter periods of history." Other rules, however, are justifiable solely by conditions that are relatively temporary (209). Why are these distinctions worth drawing? Moore never quite says. Presumably, appreciating them will facilitate a clearer and more accurate consequentialist assessment of a particular society's moral code. The utility of that code, however, rests on the social and psychological conditions that exist then and there; the extent to which they hold elsewhere is irrelevant. Thus, grounding rules on social conditions that are local or historically specific may be just as secure as basing them on conditions that hold more universally. On the other hand, of course, if the conditions on which certain moral rules rest are changing or are likely to change or if it would be feasible and beneficial to alter those conditions, then this would naturally affect consequentialist assessment of those rules.

Among the circumstances that exist only in particular states of society and that are "more or less likely to alter," Moore includes "the sanctions of legal penalties, of social disapproval, and of private remorse" (208). These all involve

---

[16] Some writers exaggerate the radicalness of Moore's stance. For example, Baldwin (1988: 131) writes that Moore "explicitly questions conventional sexual morality." What Moore explicitly questions, though, is only whether conventional sexual morality is universally valid.

important effects that must enter into consequentialist calculation. Although he believes that actions that are not independently wrong should be free of social penalties, Moore argues that where such penalties do exist they are a chief part of the moral justification (and not merely the prudential motivation) for acting in certain ways. This is because "the punishment [for a certain action] is in general itself a greater evil than would have been caused by the omission of the action punished." Indeed, Moore maintains that the prospect of punishment can be an "adequate reason for regarding an action as generally wrong, even though it has no other bad effects but even slightly good ones" (208–9).

Designating an action as being generally wrong because society punishes it is perilously close to circular reasoning: for one cannot cogently appeal to the existing structure of legal penalties and social disapproval to validate society's having the rules that give rise to that structure in the first place. Of course, if Moore is thinking only of the rightness or wrongness of individual actions in a given social framework, then there is no circularity. But this would then imply that Moore has lost the thread of his own argument because he is supposed to be showing that some commonsense moral rules can be justified by temporary or local conditions that exist only in particular states of society. Indeed, he explicitly asserts that among "the temporary conditions" that can justify social rules are "the so-called *sanctions*" (48).

5.1.3 Rules Not Generally Observed

Although it is possible "to prove a definite utility in most of those [rules] which are in general both recognised and practised" in our society, "a great part of ordinary moral exhortation and social discussion consists in the advocating of rules, which are *not* generally practised" (209). These rules suffer from three main defects, which make it unlikely that one can establish their general utility.

The first defect is that the rule requires actions that are "impossible for most individuals to perform by any volition." It presupposes "a peculiar disposition, which is given to a few and cannot even be acquired" (209). Yet, Moore argues, we do not regard something as a moral rule unless almost everyone can perform the required action if only he or she wills to do so. The second defect is that even when people are able to follow the rule, the good effects of their doing so presuppose conditions that do not exist. "A rule, of which the observance would produce good effects, if human nature were in other respects different from what it is, is advocated as if its general observance would produce the same effects now and at once" (210). The third defect is that the rule's utility depends on conditions that are likely to alter or on conditions that it would be easier or more desirable to change than it would be to bring about general adherence to the proposed rule.

Moore refrains from concrete examples, but presumably a rule that told us always to turn the other cheek or to give away our worldly possessions would exemplify the first defect because, human nature being what it is, few people could live up to it. What Moore in a later essay, "The Nature of Moral Philosophy," calls "ideal rules" also suffer from this defect (Moore 2005b: 142). Unlike rules telling us to act or refrain from acting in certain ways, ideal rules concern our inner lives. They instruct us how we should feel – commanding us, for example, to love our enemies or not to covet our neighbor's possessions. But feelings such as love or covetousness are not subject to our control in the relatively direct way in which our conduct toward enemies and neighbors is. In that essay, Moore does not deny that ideal rules are moral rules; he simply distinguishes them from "rules of duty," which tell us how to act and to which most people can adhere if they choose to.

In *Principia*, Moore seems to assume that a rule that most people cannot or will not observe lacks utility. But both there and in "The Nature of Moral Philosophy" he writes that people who have the necessary disposition should do what the rule says, even though this is beyond most people. This suggests that it would be desirable for one to be the kind of person who could live up to the rule. If so, then there could be utility in promulgating certain ideal or unrealistic rules to encourage people to act as if they had the recommended feelings and motivations and to take what steps they can to become the kind of person who does have them. On the other hand, if an ideal rule or a very onerous rule of duty sets a standard that few, if any, can reach, then attempting to establish such a rule (by, say, publicly endorsing it, trying to internalize it ourselves, and criticizing those who fail to live up to it) could prove futile or even counterproductive. Whether this risk outweighs the possible gains from endorsing an ideal or extremely burdensome rule will depend on the circumstances and the particular rule in question. One cannot exclude categorically and without empirical investigation, as *Principia* attempts to do, the possibility of upholding such rules on consequentialist grounds.

The above remarks apply equally well to the claim that the second and third defects will typically or frequently undermine the usefulness of rules that are not already generally followed. Although, again, Moore provides no examples, the good effects of some rules we are exhorted to follow probably do depend (i) on conditions that are far from widespread, (ii) on human nature being other than it is, or (iii) on circumstances that are likely to change or that it would be better or easier to change than it would be to get people to observe the rule. These factors and other related considerations could well dampen the prospective utility of some proposed moral rules. Moore's concerns are therefore perfectly relevant and legitimate. Again, though, complex empirical issues are at stake, and consequentialists should not be too quick to decide from their armchairs which rules it would be useful to promulgate and which not.

For his own part, Moore believes that the three defects he points to militate strongly against "proposed changes in social custom, [which are] advocated as being better rules to follow than those now actually followed." And, indeed, he concludes that "it seems doubtful whether Ethics can establish the utility of any rules other than those generally practised" (210). This is certainly Moore at his most conservative. However, he attempts to palliate this conservative stance by arguing that our inability to establish the utility of new rules "is fortunately of little practical moment." Even if a new rule would have greater utility, this fact will have no impact on individual conduct. This is for two reasons: (1) The individual cannot bring about general observance of the rule, and (2) the fact that its general observance would be useful gives no reason to conclude that, absent that observance, the rule ought to be obeyed (210).

Moore's first point is basically correct. Except in the most fanciful circumstances, an individual cannot bring about general observance of a new rule by his or her own action. Nevertheless, that action might encourage the future following of the rule by others (as well as the agent himself), and this effect might be significant enough to make this the agent's best course of action. In addition, an individual might be able to join with others in successfully advocating collective adherence to the new rule. With regard to his second point, there certainly are cases where obeying a new rule would be bootless unless or until a certain level of compliance is reached. On the other hand, following a new and superior rule, in the absence of some other general rule or even in the teeth of current practice, might have beneficial consequences regardless of what others generally do.

Consequentialists appropriately treat as irrelevant to moral deliberation the good results that would come from observing a proposed rule when those results are premised on counterfactual suppositions or unrealistic expectations about how people are likely to act. This is the true and insightful kernel of Moore's critique of defects two and three and of his argument that the hypothetical utility that a currently unobserved rule would have if it were to be generally followed has little bearing on how one ought to act. Thus, he is correct that there are good reasons for viewing skeptically the advocacy of moral rules that people do not now follow. These reasons, however, are less conclusive than he thinks, and his brusque dismissal of such rules is premature.

5.2 Individual Moral Choice

Moore holds that we can establish the utility of some of the basic rules of commonsense morality, but what does this imply for individual moral agents?

What role should rules play in their decision making? We turn now to Moore's answers to these questions, examining first situations in which there is a generally reliable rule and then situations where there is no such rule.

5.2.1 No Exceptions

Even if a rule is generally useful, following it will not always produce the best results, and "in some cases the neglect of an established rule will probably be the best course of action possible" (211). This conclusion suggests that consequentialists should be prepared to violate a generally useful rule whenever doing so will maximize good. Moore, however, maintains to the contrary that "the individual can ... be confidently recommended *always* to conform to rules which are both generally useful and generally practised" (213). Now, strictly speaking, what consequentialists should recommend that people do and what an individual consequentialist should choose to do can sometimes diverge. But Moore is not seeking to exploit this potential gap. He forthrightly asserts that the individual is never "justified in assuming that his is one of these exceptional cases" in which disregarding a generally useful and generally observed rule will bring more good than would obeying it (211).

This is because if observing the rule is useful in the vast majority of cases, then there is a large probability that sticking to it in the present case will be the best course of action. Because we can predict only poorly the consequences of our actions, it is doubtful that an individual's judgment that violating a rule will be beneficial can outweigh the general probability that any action of that kind will prove wrong (211–2). In addition, such judgments will generally be biased by our own desire for the results we hope to obtain by breaking the rule (212). Therefore, we ought always to observe generally useful rules, not because doing so will be right in every particular case, but because

> in *any* particular case the probability of its being so is greater than that of our being likely to decide rightly that we have before us an instance of its disutility. In short, though we may be sure that there are cases where the rule should be broken, we can never know which those cases are, and ought, therefore, never to break it. (212)

Moore's reasoning supports his conclusion, but fails to prove it. In the pertinent case, the moral agent is claiming to know something about the particular circumstances that makes it reasonable to believe that better results would come from ignoring the rule than from following it. That is, the agent believes that because what is usually the case is not now the case, the probabilities have changed. True, the stronger the evidence we have, say, that telling the truth produces more good than lying and the more instances we know in which lying misfired or had poor results, the less willing we should be to conclude that lying would be preferable to telling the truth in the present situation. And it may be, as Moore thinks, that we can be more confident in our beliefs about the typical consequences of certain types of actions than we can be in our beliefs about the specific consequences of individual actions. Moore makes a good point, too, that whenever one decides that one is justified in making an exception to a valid moral rule, there is a real danger that self-interest or personal preference will have distorted one's judgment. But although these points wisely counsel caution, they do not show that the odds are always stacked against successfully identifying exceptions to established rules.

Moore offers a further and distinct consideration in favor of his no-exceptions stance – namely, that even if one knew that in some particular situation breaking a generally useful rule would be better in other respects than adhering to it, one's doing so would set a bad example. "So far as our example has any effect at all in encouraging similar action," Moore writes, "it will certainly tend to encourage breaches of the rule which are not advantageous" (212). What will be impressed upon the imagination of others are not the exceptional circumstances that justify our action, but its resemblance to actions that really are wrongful. It sets a bad precedent for ourselves, too. Having once acted in a way that is usually wrong, one will be more likely to do so in circumstances that do not warrant it: "It is impossible for any one to keep his intellect and sentiments so clear, but that, if he has once approved of a generally wrong action, he will be more likely to approve of it also under other circumstances than those which justified it in the first instance" (213). However, although consequentialists should be aware of these problems, it seems exaggerated to hold that the risk of setting a bad example for others or a dangerous precedent for ourselves requires us always to defer to the rule even when we reasonably believe that doing so will have poor results.

Moore not only argues that one should always obey useful, generally observed rules but also defends punishing those who violate them even if that was the right thing for the person to have done and even if it was unlikely to set a bad example:

> It is undoubtedly well to punish a man, who has done an action, right in his case but generally wrong, even if his example would not be likely to have a dangerous effect. For sanctions have, in general, much more influence upon conduct than example; so that the effect of relaxing them in an exceptional case will almost certainly be an encouragement of similar action in cases which are not exceptional. (213)

An illustration might clarify Moore's point. Imagine that the injunction not to park in places officially reserved for drivers with disabilities is a valid moral rule in a certain society. Although far from the most serious moral rule, most people in that society would feel some guilt about violating it and would criticize those few drivers who do so. Now, we can imagine situations in which it would maximize good for an able-bodied driver to violate this rule (either because no disabled driver happens to need the parking space or because the benefits of the violation outweigh the inconvenience suffered by the driver with a disability). Although she understands these facts, a traffic judge, even though a consequentialist, might justifiably refuse to waive the fine in order to reinforce the general norm. Punishing the able-bodied driver will help discourage both the driver and others from violating this rule whenever they calculate that doing so would be utility maximizing – a pattern of behavior that could destroy the practice of reserving parking spaces for handicapped drivers.

Thus, from a consequentialist perspective, punishing deviation from a rule in order to bolster general adherence to it might be the best course of conduct open to us even if we believe the agent was right to have violated the rule. Whether this will always be the case, as Moore implies, is debatable. Still, what is important to bear in mind is that consequentialists are dealing with three distinct and independent issues: whether a given moral rule is justified, whether an agent would be justified in breaking that rule, and whether the agent should be punished for a justified violation of it.

5.2.2 Beyond Rules

Although Moore believes that individuals should always conform to rules that are generally useful and generally followed, the practical implications of his position are less conservative than they might appear. This is because such rules are few. Not all generally observed rules are useful ones, and we are unlikely to establish the utility of any rule not already generally observed. As a result, much of our conduct and many of the decisions we must make fall outside the scope of any binding rule. Moore probably insisted so confidently that one must always obey certain core rules just because those rules are limited in number and their domain of jurisdiction circumscribed. By contrast, when we consider "rules of which the general observance *would* be useful but does not exist, or … rules which are generally practised but which are not useful," the situation is entirely different, and "no such universal recommendations [of obedience] can be made" (213).

In the case of rules that lack utility but are nonetheless generally recognized and followed, the fact that punishment may greet one's failure to conform can be a decisive reason for compliance. Independent of this, there is "a strong probability in favor of adherence to an existing custom, even if it be a bad one" (213). This is because the fact that society generally follows a certain rule may give conforming actions a utility and nonconforming actions a disutility they would not otherwise have. The current rule and accompanying social practices may have so structured individual expectations that little, if any, good will come from contravening the rule. For example, in a society where certain kinds of theft are the common rule, the utility of a single individual refraining from such theft is doubtful even though the rule is a bad one (213). Moreover, because even poor rules can form part of the fabric of a stable society, one ought to be careful about breaking them (Harrison, 1979: 24).

Nevertheless, if the rule lacks utility, the probability in favor of adhering to it is not necessarily greater than "that of the individual's power to judge that an exception will be useful" (213). This is certainly so if "the rule which he proposes to follow, *would* be better than that which he proposes to break, *if* it were generally observed." In this case, "the effect of his example, so far as it tends to break down the existing custom, will here be for the good" (214). However, as we have seen, cases "where another rule would certainly be better than that generally observed" are "very rare" (214).

More generally, aside from "rules which are both generally practised and strongly sanctioned among us," it is extremely improbable, Moore believes, that "any general rule with regard to the utility of an action will be correct" (214). This is "the chief principle" to be taken into account when discussing the considerations that should guide one's ethical choices. Arguments can be found both for and against the various and often conflicting moral rules that are recommended to us but that are not socially established. "The most that can be said for the contradictory principles which are urged by moralists of different schools as universal duties," Moore writes, is that they "point out actions which, for persons of particular character and in particular circumstances, would and do lead to a balance of good" (214–5). Even if one succeeds in identifying the particular circumstances that would render certain kinds of actions generally advisable for certain kinds of people, Moore argues, this "would not give us, what moral laws are usually supposed to be—rules it would be desirable for every one, or even for most people, to follow" (215).

Moore also wants to challenge the assumption of most moralists that "in the matter of actions or habits of action, usually recognized as duties or virtues, it is desirable that every one should be alike" (215). As we saw earlier, Moore's discussion of virtue emphasized that only empirical investigation can determine whether a given disposition is a virtue, and it underscored the point that what is a virtue in one society may not be a virtue in another. Moore is now adding that it is not desirable for everyone in the same society to cultivate the same virtues. Rather, "the principle of division of labour, according to special capacity, which is recognised in respect of employments, would also give a better result in respect of virtues" (215).

Putting aside for a moment this intriguing contention, let us return to the larger question: How should one act when no useful rule governs the situation (bearing in mind that the utility of any rule not already generally followed is doubtful)? Moore's answer is straightforward: The agent should simply "guide his choice by a direct consideration of the intrinsic value or vileness of the effects which his action may produce" (215; cf. 48). In other words, if there is no useful, generally observed moral rule to follow, then the individual must decide what to do on the basis of direct act-consequentialist evaluation of the alternatives.[17] Moore does, however, propose three principles furnishing the individual with some guidance.

5.2.3 Three Action-Guiding Principles

When considering the outcomes of rival courses of action, a consequentialist must compare not only their goodness but also the probability of one's achieving them. Moore stresses, in particular, that if the difference in probability is sufficient, a lesser but more likely good will be a worthier target than a greater though less probable good. This fact, he argues, underwrites "the general truth" of three practical principles.

FIRST PRINCIPLE. Moore's first practical principle is that we do better to aim at a lesser good for which we have a strong preference rather than at an objectively greater good that moves us less. The reason is simple. "Natural inclination renders it immensely more easy to attain that for which such inclination is felt" (216). A critic might object that Moore's first principle incorrectly treats the actor's own inclinations as a given, as a brute fact outside his or her control, thus viewing them as if they were an external factor like the weather, which shapes, independently of one's will, the environment one faces. In defense of Moore, though, one could concede that people can act contrary to their inclinations and preferences (or at least their immediate or first-order preferences), but yet insist that one cannot turn a blind eye to any features of the world (including one's own inclinations) that will affect the likely results of rival courses of action.

---

[17] Thus, J. J. C. Smart was dead wrong to assert that "Moore argued on act-utilitarian grounds that one should never in concrete cases think as an act-utilitarian" (Smart, 1973: 43–4).

Our character is not entirely beyond our control, and our present choices and actions can and do influence our future desires and inclinations. Consequentialists will want to formulate policies and recommend practical guidelines that acknowledge these elementary facts. The question, then, is whether Moore's first principle will foster complacency about our own characters and too great a readiness to acquiesce in our present inclinations and motivations. If promulgating Moore's first principle leads people to settle too quickly for lesser goods instead of rising above their current dispositions and striving for worthier ones, then following it would fail to maximize utility.

This issue is not easy to resolve, but we can see more than a kernel of truth in Moore's principle if we connect it to his point, touched on earlier, that with regard to "actions or habits of action, usually recognised as duties or virtues, it is [not] desirable that every one should be alike" (215). Some people are better equipped and more inclined to promote the good in certain ways than in others. Acknowledging this diversity may do more to advance total good than will regimentation of purpose and goal. Volunteering at the local children's hospital, for example, might make the world better than would teaching a class on French cooking at one's country club, but that would not necessarily make it an appropriate commitment for those whose temperament leads them to enjoy haute cuisine more than children.

SECOND PRINCIPLE. Moore's concern with the effects of people's inclinations on the success of their pursuits carries over into his second principle, namely, that one should aim at goods affecting oneself and those in whom one has a strong personal interest rather than "attempt a more extended beneficence" (216). Because we strongly prefer goods that touch us and those we care about, our interests and energies are engaged, and we are more likely to succeed in attaining them. Thus, "in the immense majority of cases the best thing we can do is to aim at securing some good in which we are concerned" (216). Although not mentioned by Moore, we are also particularly well situated to realize intrinsic goods that directly affect us and those in our immediate circle because in general we have a more accurate understanding of what goods it is possible to attain, and by which means, and their achievement is more directly within our power.

We saw earlier that Moore firmly rejects egoism as a normative theory, but in elaborating his second principle, he now states that "Egoism is undoubtedly superior to Altruism as a doctrine of means" (216). This is egoism understood as a policy, not as a criterion of right. Because it understands self-interest to include not only one's purely self-regarding concerns but also the interests of those, such as one's friends, family, colleagues, and neighbors, with whom one feels some special connection, some call this "extended egoism" or "self-referential altruism" as opposed to "narrow egoism" (Mackie, 1977: 132). Whether understood narrowly or more broadly, self-interest is, of course, a strong and enduring motivation, and to preach an abstract altruism that ignores this basic fact may prove futile. Thus, although no invisible hand guides the moral world, allowing and, indeed, encouraging people to pursue goods that affect them and those who are near and dear to them may be an efficacious route to overall good.

No doubt, a policy of urging people to pursue broader rather than narrower egoistic concerns makes sense on consequentialist grounds. But is it superior to a policy that advocates altruistic conduct of a more general sort? Moore evidently believes so, and there are some reasons for thinking he might be right. People's personal attachments are inevitably limited, and the circle of those for whom we can genuinely care, and with whom we can share the goods of deep personal affection, is restricted. In addition, pragmatic considerations strongly favor concentrating our energies on goods that affect those nearby, whom we know and whose participation in those goods we are well placed to assist.

Still, consequentialists will worry that in promoting egoism, whether understood narrowly or broadly, we ignore those circumstances where encouraging more altruistic motivation might have better results. Even egoism in an extended sense seems to invite moral complacency because it overlooks the fact that our choices can affect others who are outside our network of friends, family, colleagues, and neighbors. For this reason, many consequentialists favor expanding our circle of concern beyond those intimates for whom we already care and with whom our lives are already intertwined. For one thing, the world has changed greatly since Moore's day. Because of rapid worldwide communication and increased international ties and awareness, many of us can now have an impact on the lives of distant strangers, whose circumstances we could not, in previous decades and centuries, have known of, still less affected.

THIRD PRINCIPLE. Moore's third principle is that we should favor immediate goods over future and therefore less certain ones. If one assumes that the goods in question are of roughly equal value, then this principle is surely sound. "A thing that is really good in itself, if it exist now, has precisely the same value as a thing of the same kind which may be caused to exist in the future" (216). Moore evidently thinks we are likely to overlook this elementary fact.

The rules of morality, Moore reminds us, do not directly produce positive goods; rather, they provide the framework or social prerequisites necessary for the existence of such goods. And he warns elsewhere against the "danger of confusion between the degree in which the actual lives lived [by people] are really intrinsically better, and the degree in which there is improvement merely in the *means* for living a good life" (Moore, 2005b: 148–9). For these reasons and because so much of our time and effort are directed toward "securing the continuance of what is thus a mere means," including "the claims of industry and attention to health," Moore urges that "in cases where choice is open, the certain attainment of a present good will in general have the strongest claims upon us" (216).

On the other hand, however, sometimes people erroneously discount the future by sacrificing important future goods to lesser goods of the moment, or they lose sight of the larger picture by concentrating on present enjoyments at the expense of constructing a life of greater overall value. Are these tendencies more or less worrisome than that against which the third principle warns us? This question is difficult, and any answer to it must draw on one's theory of the good and on various psychological speculations.

All three of Moore's principles raise intriguing and important issues, but they are only practical guidelines, intended to assist our act-consequentialist deliberations. Because they are not moral rules, we are free to revise or even set them aside as the occasion requires. Moore advances them to counteract the misleading influence and emphases of other theories rather than to impose additional moral requirements on how we act. His principles underscore the importance of considering, not just what is ideally best, but also the likelihood of our achieving what we aim at.

For Moore, of course, the morally right course of action for the individual in cases where there is no relevant, generally useful (and generally accepted) rule remains the same: It is the course of action that results in at least as much net good as anything else the agent could have done. But we can be in situations where the guidelines it is wise for us to follow will instruct us not to attempt to do the thing that (were we to succeed in doing it) would be the better thing to have done, and it is to the credit of his theory that it permits us to distinguish the consequentialist criterion of right from the decision-making principles that one should follow.

The contrast between these two is even more striking when we turn from practical guidelines to moral rules. As we have seen, Moore argues for staunch adherence to certain moral rules while nevertheless retaining an act-consequentialist criterion of right and wrong. Moore's normative theory thus blends elements of both act and rule consequentialism while avoiding the difficulties that arise from adhering to either a purely act-oriented or an entirely rule-based approach. His theory appreciates the advantages of firm adherence to established, utility-maximizing rules. But because valid moral rules must be socially recognized and practiced, and not merely ideal or hypothetical, Moore avoids some problems that rule consequentialism is often thought to face (see Miller, 2009: 10–2, 16–7). And because there are few such rules, his theory retains much of the flexibility of a purely act-consequentialist approach.

Conclusion

For more than half a century, Moore's *Principia Ethica* was almost certainly the single most influential work of ethics in the English language. It propelled the discipline toward metaethical questions about the nature and possible justification of ethical judgments, and its celebrated critique of naturalism had an enduring impact on the course of philosophical ethics. The foundational task, as *Principia* saw it, was to clarify the concept of good. As we have seen, Moore famously urged that "good" is a simple notion that cannot be defined or broken down by analysis into more primitive, constituent parts. Rather, goodness is a property that is sui generis, neither reducible nor equivalent to any nonethical property, whether empirical or metaphysical. Although the adjective "good" designates a nonnatural property, those things to which it applies – the things that are good – are really existing objects or states of affairs. There is, however, no property or characteristic, other than that of being good, which is common to and distinctive of them. The failure to recognize this – the failure to appreciate that good denotes a unique, indefinable, and unanalyzable property – and thus to identify this simple notion with some other notion is what Moore dubbed "the naturalistic fallacy."

Moore undoubtedly believed that a correct understanding of the concept of good was the first task of ethics precisely because he was a consequentialist and thus believed that we have to know what is good and bad in order to know what it is right or wrong for us to do. It is an irony of intellectual history that by propelling ethics toward metaethical concerns, *Principia Ethica* encouraged the very tendencies that led philosophers to neglect its own substantive normative theory. Yet had it not been for that substantive theory – in particular, had Moore not embraced consequentialism – then he would have had little reason to insist on the priority of grasping the concept of good.

Moore's value theory, of course, sharply distinguishes his consequentialism from classical utilitarianism, the hedonism of which he rejected. Although philosophers before Moore had argued against hedonism, his use of the method of isolation for addressing questions of value was influential. He relies on it not only in criticizing hedonism but also in spelling out his own account of the main goods and evils, in developing his views on virtue, and in arguing for the principle of organic wholes, which holds that the value of a given state of affairs stands in no set relation to the values of its various components. Moore resists the demand that an account of the good be unified around one or two variables. He elaborates instead a view of good and bad that is pluralistic and unsystematic. From his perspective, it is simply a fact that there are an immense variety of intrinsically good and intrinsically bad things. Still, we will agree, he thought, that the two greatest positive goods are an appreciation of beautiful objects and the pleasures of personal affection and human interaction and that the three greatest evils are pain, hatred of what is good or beautiful, and the enjoyment or admiring contemplation of things that are evil or ugly.

In addition to these distinctive value claims, Moore develops in *Principia* and in his oft-ignored *Ethics* a normative theory that makes an important and still vital contribution to the utilitarian and consequentialist tradition. Almost every aspect of it – his brief for consequentialism, his actual-results criterion of right, his respect for the limits to our moral knowledge, his defense of certain core moral rules, and what he has to say about individual moral choice – touch on live issues, ones that are central to current debates among contemporary consequentialists and between them and their critics. Moore's normative theory therefore deserves more attention that it usually receives, which is why this Element gives it proportionally more attention than have other studies of his ethics.

This survey of Moore's ethical thought has expressed reservations about various aspects of it, but Moore's importance does not hang on whether, over a hundred years after his main work in ethics was written, philosophers agree with everything he had to say – still less on whether he said the final word in metaethics, value theory, or normative ethics. Rather, what makes Moore an important moral philosopher, one whose thought amply repays study, is that he raises fundamental questions, advances credible and often fecund and innovative answers to them – whether those answers ultimately prove satisfactory or not – and does so with a philosophical skill that is still impressive and an intellectual candor that one cannot fail to admire.[18]

---

[18] I thank Vuko Andrić, Ben Eggleston, Dale Miller, Joe Waterhouse, and an anonymous reviewer for reading so carefully and commenting so helpfully on earlier drafts of this Element.

References

Andrić, V. (2013). Objective consequentialism and the licensing dilemma. *Philosophical Studies*, **162**(3), 547–66.

Ayer, A. J. (1982). *Philosophy in the Twentieth Century*, London: Unwin.

Baldwin, T. (1988). Review of Tom Regan, *Bloomsbury's prophet*, and G. E. Moore, *The early essays*. *Mind*, **97**(385), 129–33.

Baldwin, T. (1990). *G. E. Moore*, London: Routledge.

Baldwin, T. (1993). Editor's introduction. In *Principia Ethica*, rev. ed., ed. T. Baldwin. Cambridge: Cambridge University Press, pp.ix–xxxvii.

Darwall, S. (1989). Moore to Stevenson. In R. Cavalier, J. S. Gouinlock, and J. P. Sterba, eds., *Ethics in the History of Western Philosophy*. Basingstoke: Palgrave Macmillan, pp. 366–98.

Darwall, S. (2006). How should ethics relate to (the rest of) philosophy? Moore's legacy. In T. Horgan and M. Timmons, eds., *Metaethics after Moore*. Oxford: Oxford University Press, pp. 17–37.

Ewing, A. C. (1961). G. E. Moore. *Mind*, **71**(282), 251.

Harrison, J. (1979). Rule utilitarianism and cumulative-effect utilitarianism. *Canadian Journal of Philosophy*, suppl. vol. **5**, 21–45.

Horgan, T., and Timmons, M., eds. (2006). *Metaethics after Moore*, Oxford: Oxford University Press.

Kagan, S. (1989). *The Limits of Morality*, Oxford: Oxford University Press.

Mackie, J. L. (1976). Sidgwick's pessimism. *Philosophical Quarterly*, **16**(104), 317–27.

Mackie, J. L. (1977). *Ethics: Inventing Right and Wrong*, Harmondsworth: Penguin.

Mill, J. S. (1969). *Collected Works*, vol. X, Toronto: University of Toronto Press.

Miller, R. B. (2009). Actual rule utilitarianism. *Journal of Philosophy*, **106**(1), 5–28.

Moore, G. E. (1903a). Mr. McTaggart's ethics. *International Journal of Ethics* (now *Ethics*), **13**(3), 341–70.

Moore, G. E. (1903b). Review of Franz Brentano, *The origin of the knowledge of right and wrong*. *International Journal of Ethics* (now *Ethics*), **14**(1), 115–23.

Moore, G. E. (1907–8). Review of Hastings Rashdall, *The theory of good and evil*. *Hibbert Journal*, **6**(2), 446–51.

Moore, G. E. (1952). A reply to my critics. In P. A. Schilpp, ed., *The Philosophy of G. E. Moore*, 2nd ed., New York: Tudor, pp. 535–687.

Moore, G. E. (1962 [1932]). Is goodness a quality? Reprinted in G. E. Moore, *Philosophical Papers*. New York: Collier, pp. 89–100.

Moore, G. E. (1991). *The Elements of Ethics*, ed. T. Regan, Philadelphia: Temple University Press. This a series of pre-*Principia* lectures, unpublished in Moore's lifetime.

Moore, G. E. (1993a [1922]). The conception of intrinsic value. Reprinted in G. E. Moore, *Principia Ethica*, rev. ed., ed. T. Baldwin. Cambridge: Cambridge University Press, pp. 280–98.

Moore, G. E. (1993b [1903]). *Principia Ethica*, rev. ed., ed. T. Baldwin, Cambridge: Cambridge University Press.

Moore, G. E. (2005a [1912]). *Ethics*, ed. W. H. Shaw, Oxford: Oxford University Press.

Moore, G. E. (2005b [1922]). The nature of moral philosophy. Reprinted in G. E. Moore, *Ethics*, ed. W. H. Shaw. Oxford: Oxford University Press, pp. 135–57.

Parfit, D. (2011–7). *On What Matters*, 3 vols., Oxford: Oxford University Press.

Rashdall, H. (1924). *The Theory of Good and Evil: A Treatise on Moral Philosophy*, 2nd ed., 2 vols., Oxford: Oxford University Press.

Regan, D. H. (2003). How to be a Moorean. *Ethics* **113**(3), 651–77.

Ross, W. D. (1930). *The Right and the Good*, Oxford: Oxford University Press.

Russell, B. (1904). The meaning of good. *Independent Review*, **2**(8), 328–33.

Russell, B. (1910). *Philosophical Essays*, London: Longmans, Green, & Co.

Shaw, W. H. (1995). *Moore on Right and Wrong: The Normative Ethics of G. E. Moore*, Dordrecht, The Netherlands: Kluwer.

Shaw, W. H. (1999). *Contemporary Ethics: Taking Account of Utilitarianism*, Oxford: Blackwell.

Sidgwick, H. (1966 [1907]). *The Methods of Ethics*, 7th ed., New York: Dover.

Smart, J. J. C. (1973). An outline of a system of utilitarian ethics. In J. J. C. Smart and B. Williams, *Utilitarianism: For and Against*. Cambridge: Cambridge University Press, pp. 3–74.

Smith, M. (2006). Moore on the right, the good, and uncertainty. In T. Horgan and M. Timmons, eds., *Metaethics after Moore*. Oxford: Oxford University Press, pp. 133–48.

Stevenson, C. (1952). Moore's argument against certain forms of ethical naturalism. In P. A. Schilpp, ed., *The Philosophy of G. E. Moore*, 2nd ed., New York: Tudor, pp. 71–90.

Thomson, J. J. (2001). *Goodness and Advice*, Princeton, NJ: Princeton University Press.

White, A. R. (1969). *G. E. Moore: A Critical Exposition*, Oxford: Blackwell.

Zimmerman, M. J. (2008). *Living with Uncertainty: The Moral Significance of Ignorance*, Cambridge: Cambridge University Press.

Ethics

Ben Eggleston
University of Kansas

Ben Eggleston is a professor of philosophy at the University of Kansas. He is the editor of John Stuart Mill, *Utilitarianism: With Related Remarks from Mill's Other Writings* (Hackett, 2017) and a co-editor of *Moral Theory and Climate Change: Ethical Perspectives on a Warming Planet* (Routledge, 2020), *The Cambridge Companion to Utilitarianism* (Cambridge, 2014), and *John Stuart Mill and the Art of Life* (Oxford, 2011). He is also the author of numerous articles and book chapters on various topics in ethics.

Dale E. Miller
Old Dominion University

Dale E. Miller is a professor of philosophy at Old Dominion University. He is the author of *John Stuart Mill: Moral, Social and Political Thought* (Polity, 2010) and a co-editor of *Moral Theory and Climate Change: Ethical Perspectives on a Warming Planet* (Routledge, 2020), *A Companion to Mill* (Blackwell, 2017), *The Cambridge Companion to Utilitarianism* (Cambridge, 2014), *John Stuart Mill and the Art of Life* (Oxford, 2011), and *Morality, Rules, and Consequences: A Critical Reader* (Edinburgh, 2000). He is also the editor-in-chief of *Utilitas*, and the author of numerous articles and book chapters on various topics in ethics broadly construed.

About the Series

This Elements series provides an extensive overview of major figures, theories, and concepts in the field of ethics. Each entry in the series acquaints students with the main aspects of its topic while articulating the author's distinctive viewpoint in a manner that will interest researchers.

Cambridge Elements $\equiv$

Ethics

CPSIA information can be obtained
at www.ICGtesting.com
Printed in the USA
LVHW040854280721
693861LV00006B/710

9 781108 706544